The Red Mole

Revolutionary Strategy in an Age of Organizational Crisis

Red Mole Substack

ISBN 978-0-906378-23

ABOUT THIS COLLECTION

This book brings together most of Red Mole's most-read essays from 2025, selected based on audience engagement and strategic impact. Each article was originally published as a Substack post and has been lightly edited for print formatting.

Red Mole aims to provide rigorous, historically-informed strategic analysis for revolutionary organizers and activists. We take accuracy seriously in characterizing other organizations and political positions, recognizing that credible critique requires careful evidence and fair representation. We welcome corrections to factual errors.

The views presented reflect our independent, broadly Fourth Internationalist perspective, but we seek dialogue with thoughtful left critics who disagree with our strategic assessments. Our goal is to strengthen left movements through honest analysis, not to settle ideological disputes.

For the most current Red Mole analysis and subscriber discussion, visit: RedMole.substack.com.

Book Cover by Oracle BookArt

FOLR🌹SE
PRESS

Contents

Ideological Mapping & Strategic Frameworks

Mapping the Conservative Left:
Why Some Socialists Sound Like the Right

The rise of the far-right across Europe and North America has prompted urgent soul-searching on the left. From Trump's return to power to the growth of Alternative for Germany (AfD), from Giorgia Meloni's ascendancy in Italy to the surge of Reform UK, reactionary forces are capitalizing on widespread social discontent. Yet a troubling phenomenon has emerged alongside this rightward shift: sections of the left itself have begun adopting positions that sound suspiciously similar to those of their supposed political opponents.

This "conservative left" represents a fundamental betrayal of socialist principles. Rather than offering a genuine alternative to capitalist crisis, these currents have absorbed key elements of right-wing discourse—from economic nationalism and anti-immigrant sentiment to cultural traditionalism and geopolitical authoritarianism. Understanding this phenomenon is crucial for any socialist strategy that seeks to build genuine working-class unity against our real enemies: the capitalist class and their political representatives.

The conservative left is not a monolithic bloc but encompasses several distinct, though interconnected, tendencies. These range from mainstream social democratic parties that have capitulated to neoliberalism while adopting cultural conservatism, to new "red-brown" formations that explicitly merge left

1

economics with right-wing cultural politics, to campist movements that support authoritarian regimes abroad, to identity politics backlash that fragments working-class solidarity. Each represents a different form of capitulation to the forces we should be fighting.

The "Red-Brown" Vanguard: From Wagenknecht to Galloway

The most dangerous and explicit form of conservative left politics can be seen in the emergence of "red-brown" formations—parties and movements that consciously combine left-wing economic positions with far-right cultural politics. The term "red-brown" refers to the fusion of red (socialist) economic policies with brown (fascist) cultural and nationalist positions, a toxic combination that divides the working class against itself.

Germany's Sahra Wagenknecht Alliance (BSW) represents the paradigmatic case. Formed in 2024 by former Die Linke leader Sahra Wagenknecht, the BSW has achieved significant electoral success by adopting what it calls a "left-conservative" platform. The party combines traditional left-wing positions on economic inequality and social spending with hardline stances on immigration, climate skepticism, and cultural traditionalism.

Wagenknecht's strategy is cynically calculated: she explicitly aims to "contest the electorate with the far-right" by adopting arguments "very similar to those used by the Alternative for Germany." The BSW demands strict limitations on immigration to "protect local workers and national cultural cohesion," opposes Green transition policies as threats to traditional industry, and promotes what Wagenknecht calls resistance to "lifestyle leftism"—code for opposition to LGBTQ+ rights, anti-racism, and feminist organizing.

The political logic here is devastating for working-class solidarity. As critics note, Wagenknecht's politics represent a "division of the working class itself: national workers on one side, immigrants on the other." Instead of uniting all workers against their exploitation by capital, the BSW creates an "alliance with employers" against immigrant workers, transforming class struggle into national competition.

Britain's George Galloway has pioneered similar tactics through his Workers Party of Britain. Despite its name, the party's politics combine economic populism with cultural reaction. Galloway has consistently opposed trans rights, describing transgender identity as "fashionable nonsense," while promoting what he calls "traditional family values." His party's 2024 manifesto combined calls for nationalization with opposition to "gender ideology" and promises to "end mass immigration."

Like Wagenknecht, Galloway presents this fusion as electoral pragmatism—appealing to working-class voters allegedly alienated by the mainstream left's focus on "identity politics." But this strategy fundamentally misunderstands both working-class consciousness and socialist politics. By accepting the far-right's framing of social issues, these politicians legitimize reactionary ideas while fragmenting the very class solidarity they claim to represent.

The red-brown disease can spread further without inoculation. Organizations at risk like Counterfire in Britain, while maintaining left-wing rhetoric, have consistently aligned with authoritarian positions internationally, acting as surrogates for Assad, Putin and Trump. Their opposition to supporting Ukrainian resistance and their hostility to transgender struggles reveals the logical endpoint of politics that prioritize "anti-Western" positioning over genuine solidarity with the oppressed.

Social Democratic Capitulation: The "Third Way" to Nowhere

A second strand of conservative left politics emerges from the rightward drift of mainstream social democratic parties. This represents what we might call the "Third Way" variant of conservative leftism—parties that have abandoned anti-capitalist politics while adopting increasingly conservative positions on social and cultural issues.

Tony Blair's New Labour pioneered this model, combining acceptance of neoliberal economics with authoritarian positions on law and order, immigration, and civil liberties. Blair's governments introduced detention without trial, ramped up deportations, and promoted "British values" in ways that barely differed from Conservative rhetoric. This wasn't accidental drift but conscious strategy—an attempt to triangulate between left and right that ended up legitimizing right-wing positions.

Portugal's Socialist Party (PS) offers a contemporary example. Despite its name, the PS governs as a neoliberal party that has systematically undermined public services while adopting increasingly harsh positions on immigration and law enforcement. Their policies have created the social discontent that far-right parties like Chega exploit, demonstrating how social democratic capitulation paves the way for fascist advance.

These parties represent what Marxist Antonio Gramsci would call "transformism"—the absorption of potentially oppositional forces into the existing system. By abandoning any pretense of systemic change, they become indistinguishable from explicitly capitalist parties except in their rhetoric. Their "conservatism" lies not in adopting far-right positions wholesale, but in their defensive posture that accepts capitalism as eternal while making increasingly desperate appeals to "traditional" values and national identity.

The tragedy of social democratic capitulation is that it abandons precisely the universalist vision that could unite working people across racial, national, and cultural lines. Instead of fighting for policies that materially improve life for all workers, these parties retreat into defensive nationalism that inevitably benefits the right.

Campism: When Anti-Imperialism Becomes Its Opposite

A third strand of conservative leftism emerges from what analysts call "campism"—the tendency to organize politics around support for any regime or movement that opposes "Western imperialism," regardless of its internal character or treatment of working people. Campism represents a fundamental perversion of genuine anti-imperialist politics.

Traditional campism emerged during the Cold War, when many leftists automatically supported Soviet policies regardless of their impact on workers in the USSR or internationally. Contemporary "neo-campism" follows the same logic, supporting authoritarian regimes like Putin's Russia or Xi's China simply because they challenge US hegemony, while ignoring their oppressive internal policies and imperial ambitions.

Britain's Stop the War Coalition exemplifies neo-campist politics in practice. Despite its anti-war rhetoric, StWC has consistently opposed Western support for Ukrainian resistance while remaining silent about Russian war crimes. Their analysis treats the conflict as merely a "proxy war between imperialist camps," thereby "minimizing, if not outrightly denying, Ukrainian agency" and effectively supporting Russian conquest.

This isn't genuine anti-imperialism but its opposite—support for alternative imperialisms. Real anti-imperialist politics would support the self-determination of oppressed nations like Ukraine while opposing all imperial powers, including Russia and China. Campist politics, by contrast, subordinates the struggles of oppressed peoples to geopolitical calculations about weakening "the West."

The "tankie" phenomenon represents campism's most grotesque manifestation. This online subculture, particularly strong among younger leftists, promotes a "romanticized and nostalgic view of the Soviet Union and Stalinism" through memes and social media performance. "Tankies" (named after supporters of Soviet tanks crushing Hungarian and Czech uprisings) combine aesthetic nostalgia for authoritarian socialism with contemporary support for regimes like Putin's Russia.

This "digital neo-Stalinism" reveals campism's fundamentally conservative character. Rather than learning from the failures of 20th-century socialism to build more democratic and emancipatory alternatives, tankies romanticize authoritarian models that suppressed working-class self-organization. Their politics represent not revolutionary advance but reactionary nostalgia.

Identity Politics Backlash: The "Anti-Woke" Left

The fourth strand of conservative leftism emerges from backlash against what critics call "wokism"—though this term is often weaponized to attack any politics focused on racial, gender, or sexual oppression. Nevertheless, certain trends within identity-focused organizing do exhibit genuinely conservative tendencies that fragment working-class solidarity.

The problem isn't fighting oppression based on race, gender, sexuality, or other identities—this is essential to any genuinely socialist politics. The problem lies in approaches that atomize these struggles, divorcing them from class analysis and collective action. When identity politics becomes purely individualistic and competitive, it can indeed serve conservative ends.

"Wokism," properly understood, refers to approaches that reduce complex social struggles to individual consumer choices, moral posturing, or bureaucratic representation without challenging underlying power structures. This manifests in corporate diversity initiatives that replace collective organizing, "cancel culture" that substitutes personal attacks for systemic change, and academic discourse that obscures rather than clarifies class relations.

The conservative character of such approaches lies in their compatibility with capitalist social relations. A capitalism that includes more diverse CEOs and politicians remains capitalism. Identity politics that focuses on representation within existing institutions rather than transforming those institutions ultimately serves conservative ends.

Moreover, purely individualistic identity politics can generate its own reactionary backlash. The rise of the "manosphere" among young men, with its misogynistic and anti-feminist politics, partly represents a reactionary response to perceived feminist "excesses." While this backlash is unjustifiable, its existence demonstrates how fragmented identity politics can create political space for right-wing organizing.

The solution isn't to abandon struggles against racial, gender, or sexual oppression—these are integral to working-class liberation. Instead, we need an intersectional analysis that understands how capitalism generates and reinforces multiple forms of oppression while building collective struggle that unites rather than divides working people.

The Material Roots of Conservative Leftism

These conservative left tendencies didn't emerge in a vacuum. They represent responses to real material conditions and political crises that have shaped left politics over recent decades.

The collapse of the Soviet Union and discrediting of state socialist models created an ideological vacuum that left many socialists without clear alternatives to capitalism. This crisis of imagination made left politics vulnerable to various forms of accommodation with existing power structures.

Simultaneously, the neoliberal offensive since the 1980s created what theorists call a "pincer movement" against the left: appear too radical and face marginalization; moderate your positions and become indistinguishable from liberal parties. This pressure pushed many left parties toward the kind of capitulation represented by Third Way social democracy.

The 2008 financial crisis and subsequent austerity policies generated massive social discontent but also created political instability that far-right movements have exploited more effectively than the left. This context helps explain why some leftists have adopted red-brown strategies—attempting to compete with the far-right on its own terrain rather than offering genuine alternatives.

Economic changes have also fragmented traditional working-class communities and identities, making older forms of socialist organizing more difficult. The decline of industrial employment, the rise of precarious service work, and increasing social atomization have weakened the material basis for collective working-class politics.

Finally, the dominance of social media and digital communication has created new forms of political engagement that often prioritize performance over substance, individual expression over collective action, and ideological purity over strategic effectiveness. This context has enabled both tankie subcultures and individualistic identity politics.

Beyond Conservative Leftism: A Socialist Alternative

Understanding conservative leftism's material roots suggests strategies for overcoming it. Rather than simply condemning these tendencies, we need to build genuine alternatives that address the real problems they attempt to solve while maintaining socialist principles.

First, we need to rebuild a genuinely internationalist politics that supports oppressed peoples everywhere without subordinating their struggles to geopolitical calculations. This means supporting Ukrainian self-determination while opposing NATO expansion, defending Palestinian liberation while criticizing antisemitism, and building solidarity across borders while fighting our own ruling classes.

Second, we must develop an intersectional class politics that understands how capitalism generates multiple forms of oppression while building collective struggle that unites rather than divides working people. This requires fighting racism, sexism, and other forms of oppression not as separate issues but as integral aspects of capitalist domination.

Third, we need to articulate a positive vision of socialist democracy that learns from past failures while offering genuine alternatives to both capitalism and authoritarianism. This means promoting worker democracy, ecological sustainability, and social liberation as interconnected goals.

Fourth, we must rebuild working-class organization from the ground up, creating new forms of collective action appropriate to contemporary conditions while learning from historical experiences. This requires patient organizing work that builds real power rather than performative politics.

Finally, we need to develop media and communication strategies that counter both mainstream propaganda and social media manipulation while promoting genuine political education and collective action.

The stakes couldn't be higher. As fascist movements gain strength globally, the left faces a choice: continue fragmenting into conservative dead-ends or unite around genuinely emancipatory politics. The conservative left represents the path to defeat—dividing workers against each other while legitimizing right-wing ideas. Only by understanding and overcoming these tendencies can we build the united, international working-class movement necessary to defeat both capitalism and fascism.

The alternative to conservative leftism isn't moderation or accommodation—it's revolutionary politics that takes seriously both the material conditions of working-class life and the emancipatory potential of collective struggle. This is the socialism we need: internationalist, anti-capitalist, democratic, and uncompromisingly committed to the liberation of all oppressed peoples.

Further reading

Here are five articles that directly address our topic:

- "Do conservadorismo de esquerda ao comunismo ácido" by Diogo Machado: This article directly defines and analyzes "esquerdas conservadoras", differentiating them into two faces of capitulation: the 'third way' (e.g., Tony Blair/PS) which is a surrender to neoliberalism, and the 'conservative left' (e.g., Wagenknecht) which incorporates the cultural agenda of the far-right. It argues that a purely social-democratic platform is inherently conservative as it lacks structural change, and criticizes a focus on immediate proposals within a capitalist grammar as a renunciation of the fight for cultural hegemony and structural alternatives. Machado advocates for "acid communism" as a radical, creative, and collective political imaginary.

- "As duas identidades da esquerda etiquetária" by Francisco Louçã: This article identifies campism and sectarianism as the defining characteristics of the conservative left. It explains how campism, originating from the Cold War alignment with the USSR, persists today in supporting any regime hostile to the US, even if it's an "autocratic and plutocratic" one like Putin's Russia. This alignment leads to "insanable contradictions" and a succession of compromises with various regimes. The article further argues that sectarianism, fueled by virtual social networks, deforms political discourse and isolates the left from potential allies in social struggles.

- "Novos tankies e o neoestalinismo digital: como é incubada a Esquerda Conservadora" by João Bernardo Narciso: This article explores the phenomenon of "new tankies," young leftists romantically nostalgic for the Soviet Union and Stalinism. It explains how online platforms, particularly social media, foster this subculture through uniform cultural patterns, memes, and shock tactics that oversimplify complex historical and theoretical analyses. This digital socialization, often disconnected from real collective activism, leads to "purismos ideológicos e identitarismos políticos" and prioritizes principle affirmation over collective action, thereby risking the left's potential to unite and win."

- "Wokismo". O conservadorismo de esquerda que a direita prefere" by Ana

Vasquez and Hugo Monteiro: This piece argues that a certain type of "wokism," as perceived and often weaponized by the right, constitutes a form of "conservative left". It suggests that when the "woke" designation becomes a comfortable classification that depoliticizes positions, isolates demands, and frames claims in a competitive manner, it becomes suitable for a right-wing common sense. The authors, citing Susan Neiman, critique an approach that confines each oppressed group to the "prism of its own marginalization," reducing social struggle to a private, particular criterion that approaches a "conservative dogmatic" stance. It emphasizes that this individualistic, competitive approach neglects class alliances and collective action necessary for anticapitalist struggle.

- "Qual é a nossa pátria? - crítica do nacionalismo de esquerda" by Daniel Borges: This article critiques "nacionalismo de esquerda" (left-wing nationalism), arguing that its "mortal sin" is confusing its political subjects. It uses the example of Sahra Wagenknecht's politics in Germany, which, under the guise of recentering workers' struggles, divides the working class by prioritizing national workers over immigrants. This approach is seen as a "movement of resistance to globalization and cultural transformations," which, by forming a coalition of workers and employers against immigrant workers, effectively aligns with conservative and divisive policies. It concludes that while anti-colonial movements have historically used the national question for liberation, a "critique of left-wing nationalism is nothing more than a critique of a divisive policy".

These five recommended articles – all appeared in Anticapitalista #78, published in January 2025.

This particular issue marked a significant change for Anticapitalista, as it was "renovated" with its entire space dedicated to reflective texts. The primary goal of this new format is to deepen debate within the Bloco de Esquerda, explore new questions, and offer fresh approaches to enduring themes, ultimately contributing to the questioning of dogmas and the construction of a socialist ideology for the future. The central theme of this special issue, which these five articles directly address, was "Anatomia das Esquerdas conservadoras" (Anatomy of Conservative Lefts).

Strategic Lessons: Why Cliff & Kidron's "International Socialism" Tradition Gets Permanent Revolution Wrong

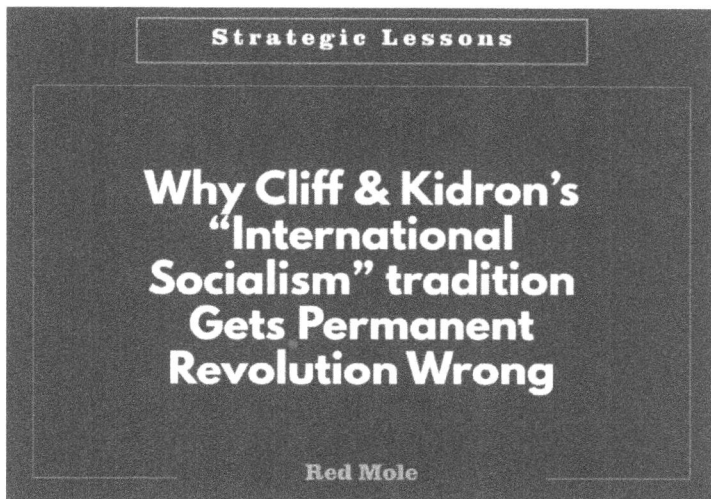

Nepal's revolutionary experience poses fundamental questions about how revolutionary theory applies to 21st-century conditions. A recent discussion with Andy Wilson (formerly of the IST tradition) and Nigel Incitegema (a member of Rise, the Fourth Internationalist current in Ireland) illuminates deeper strategic divisions within the international left—not about whether to support working-class independence, but about how revolutionary transformation can succeed under contemporary conditions.

Wilson raises the classical IST challenge: Nepal lacks the concentrated industrial proletariat that characterized Russia's revolutionary centers like the Putilov works. Without massive factory concentrations, can permanent revolution theory apply? Meanwhile, Incitegema poses the geopolitical realism question: even if revolutionary leadership emerges, can small countries like Nepal resist economic strangulation by hostile neighbors?

Both challenges reflect how dramatically global capitalism has transformed since Trotsky formulated permanent revolution theory. The question isn't whether these theorists support working-class independence—both traditions do—but whether classical revolutionary strategy remains viable.

What the IST Actually Predicted About Nepal

The IST tradition's Deflected Permanent Revolution (DPR) theory predicted exactly what occurred in Nepal. Tony Cliff's framework anticipated that peasant-based revolutionary movements led by non-proletarian forces would achieve democratic tasks (abolishing monarchy, ending feudalism) but stop short of establishing genuine working-class power.

Nepal validates this prediction perfectly: the CPN (Maoist) successfully overthrew the monarchy and landlord system, then transformed into a conventional parliamentary party competing for government positions. As the PDF analysis notes, "it did not usher in a socialist state. Instead, it transitioned into a mainstream political party, engaging in the very parliamentary politics it once rejected."

The IST would argue this outcome was structurally inevitable given the movement's class composition and leadership. Without organized working-class leadership from the outset, revolutionary movements become vehicles for new elite formation rather than genuine social transformation.

Where Both Theories Struggle with Contemporary Reality
THE IST'S ANALYTICAL LIMITATION

While the IST correctly predicted Nepal's trajectory, their theory offers no strategic alternative. If working-class organization remains too weak to lead revolutionary transformation, what political strategy makes sense? The IST's descriptive accuracy becomes strategically paralyzing—they can explain why revolutions fail but cannot propose how they might succeed under unfavorable conditions.

Wilson's question about the "missing Putilov works" reflects this limitation. The IST recognizes that Nepal's working class lacks the concentration and organization that enabled Bolshevik success, but offers little or no framework for building revolutionary capacity under different conditions.

FOURTH INTERNATIONAL'S STRATEGIC DILEMMA

The Fourth International faces the opposite problem. Permanent revolution theory provides strategic direction—working-class leadership of democratic struggles advancing toward socialism—but struggles with the practical question of implementation when working-class organization remains embryonic, and other alternatives are hegemonic.

Incitegema's geographic fatalism highlights this challenge: even successful revolutionary leadership faces immediate economic strangulation by hostile neighbors. How does permanent revolution strategy address this practical constraint?

Nepal's Distributed Working Class: Beyond Factory Concentration

Both theoretical traditions underestimate how global capitalism has restructured working-class formation. Nepal's working class isn't absent—it's globally distributed. Approximately 3.5 million Nepalese workers labor abroad, primarily in Malaysia and Gulf states, remitting $11 billion annually (26.6% of GDP).

This international proletariat experiences classic exploitation: construction, manufacturing, domestic labor under brutal conditions. Their remittances exceed Nepal's entire industrial output, making them economically central to the country's reproduction.

Historical precedent supports this analysis. The 1947 Biratnagar Jute Mill Strike demonstrated how small industrial concentrations could trigger national transformation. A local labor dispute rapidly became a nationwide anti-regime movement that "shattered the political status quo."

Revolutionary potential lies not in concentrated heavy industry but in politically conscious workers occupying strategic economic positions—whether in Nepal's limited industrial sectors or the international labor circuits that sustain the domestic economy.

Strategic Synthesis: Learning from Theoretical Limitations
WHAT THE IST GETS RIGHT

The DPR framework correctly identifies why non-working class revolutionary leadership produces "deflected" outcomes. Nepal's experience confirms that peasant-based movements, however militant, cannot establish sustainable working-class power without genuine proletarian organization and leadership.

The CPN (Maoist) decline validates this analysis: their initial success came from mobilizing the rural poor against combined feudal-capitalist oppression, but their trajectory toward parliamentary accommodation was predictable given their class base and political leadership.

WHAT FOURTH INTERNATIONAL TRADITION OFFERS

Permanent revolution theory provides strategic coherence that DPR lacks. Rather than simply explaining revolutionary failure, it offers a framework for building working-class leadership capable of completing democratic tasks while advancing toward socialist transformation.

The theory's emphasis on international strategy directly addresses Incitegema's geographic constraints. Revolutionary leadership in small countries must build international working-class connections from the outset, not treat internationalism as a luxury for after domestic victory.

Contemporary Applications

Nepal's distributed working class actually strengthens the permanent revolution framework. Unlike 1917 Russia's nationally contained proletariat, Nepal's workers are already internationally organized through migration networks. Revolutionary strategy should build on these existing connections rather than waiting for domestic industrial development.

The environmental crisis adds strategic urgency. Countries like Nepal face catastrophic climate impacts requiring rapid economic transformation that only revolutionary strategy can achieve. Market mechanisms and parliamentary gradualism cannot address the scale of necessary change.

Strategic Lessons for Red Mole Readers

First: Both the IST and Fourth International traditions offer partial insights but struggle with contemporary conditions. The IST correctly diagnoses why revolutions fail but provides no alternative strategy. The FI offers strategic direction but arguably underestimates practical constraints.

Second: Nepal's experience demonstrates that "realistic" compromise strategies systematically fail. The CPN (Maoist) followed exactly the parliamentary path that both traditions would critique—entering coalitions, moderating demands, accepting institutional constraints. The result is continuing neoliberal governance and mass disillusionment.

Third: Modern working classes exist in forms classical theory didn't anticipate. Revolutionary organizations must develop new approaches to international working-class organization rather than waiting for "proper" industrial concentration.

Contemporary relevance: These lessons directly challenge European left formations following Wilson's logic. From France's coalition strategies to Spain's parliamentary alliances, the pattern repeats: initial enthusiasm for "broad democratic" unity followed by systematic betrayal of working-class interests when bourgeois coalition partners demand "responsibility."

As Phil Hearse demonstrates, this isn't tactical failure but theoretical inevitability. Any strategy that subordinates working-class independence to broader "democratic" alliances will eventually prioritize maintaining those alliances over advancing working-class interests. Nepal's CPN (Maoist) trajectory from revolutionary insurgency to neoliberal management is the contemporary expression of this historical pattern.

The DPR-Fatalism Connection: Wilson's position exemplifies how apparently sophisticated theoretical analysis becomes a rationalization for strategic passivity. By emphasizing Nepal's lack of industrial concentration, the IST approach transforms revolutionary theory from a guide to building working-class power into an explanation for why such power remains impossible.

This is the deeper significance of Andy Wilson's current position as someone who "no longer sees himself as a Marxist of any sort." The IST's economic determinism can lead logically to abandoning revolutionary intervention entirely when objective conditions appear unfavorable—exactly the fatalism Hearse identifies in two-stage theory generally.

Nepal's class struggle continues. The question is whether revolutionary leadership will emerge to organize the working class that exists internationally, not the concentrated industrial proletariat that historical precedent suggests should exist domestically.

A Critical Excavation of Stalinism's Internal Contradictions

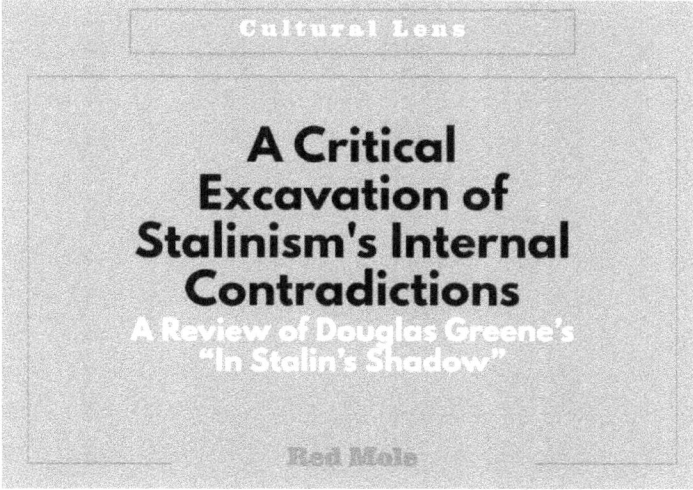

Douglas Greene's In Stalin's Shadow stands out as a deeply researched examination of Stalinism that goes well beyond conventional historical accounts. Rather than simply recounting events, the book thoughtfully unpacks the myths surrounding Soviet politics and offers profound insights into political resistance, ideological shifts, and the challenging task of interpreting contested histories.

Greene approaches his subject with careful reflection on the methodological challenges historians face when dealing with politically charged topics. His work pays particular attention to the high personal and political costs borne by those who opposed Stalin, spotlighting figures such as Martemyan Riutin, who bravely contested Stalin's leadership within the Communist Party in the early 1930s.

Drawing from extensive archival material and a materialist analytical framework, Greene illuminates the complex struggles within the Soviet bureaucracy and highlights political opposition often overlooked by mainstream narratives. A key feature of the book is its detailed critique of modern Stalinist apologetics, where Greene carefully examines and challenges the positions of scholars like Domenico Losurdo and Grover Furr.

Moving beyond simplistic portraits of Stalin as a lone dictator, the book engages with revisionist historians such as J. Arch Getty and Sheila Fitzpatrick to depict Stalin as a nuanced political actor navigating a turbulent bureaucratic landscape. Greene's analysis offers a sophisticated perspective on totalitarianism, emphasizing the contradictions and internal dynamics of the Soviet system rather than relying on mechanical labels.

Perhaps most compelling are the individual stories of disillusionment and courage. Through the experiences of activists like Walter Krivitsky, who risked everything to uphold his principles, and Peggy Dennis, whose emotional response to the Soviet Secret Speech reveals the human toll of repression, Greene provides intimate windows into the broader political context.

The work also addresses the methodological hurdles of studying revolutionary history, acknowledging the difficulties in translating revolutionary experiences across different contexts. He critiques both Stalinist defenders and staunch anti-communists for their analytical limitations, demonstrating the complex challenges posed by state censorship and historical information suppression.

While the book's dense theoretical discussions and archival depth may appeal more to academic readers, it offers invaluable insights for anyone interested in the complexities of Soviet political history. It moves beyond merely refuting conspiracies to offer a thoughtful, nuanced examination of power, bureaucracy, and historical memory.

Ultimately, In Stalin's Shadow is a profound reflection on political integrity, resistance, and the human costs of authoritarianism. Greene resists the urge to present a neat, definitive narrative, instead inviting readers into a detailed and multifaceted exploration of one of the 20th century's most complex political landscapes.

For historians, political theorists, and readers curious about rigorous historical methodology, this book is an indispensable contribution. Greene masterfully illuminates the personal dimensions of political struggle, showing how ideological commitments are tested, reshaped, or broken under systemic oppression.

Far more than a history book, In Stalin's Shadow challenges us to reconsider how political movements and historical interpretations evolve, making it essential reading for those grappling with the legacies of totalitarianism.

HOW TO ORDER

In Stalin's Shadow is published by Resistance Books:
https://resistancebooks.org/product/in-stalins-shadow-leon-trotsky-and-the-legacy-of-the-moscow-trials/

The Fourth International: From activist origins, through splits, to theoretical growth

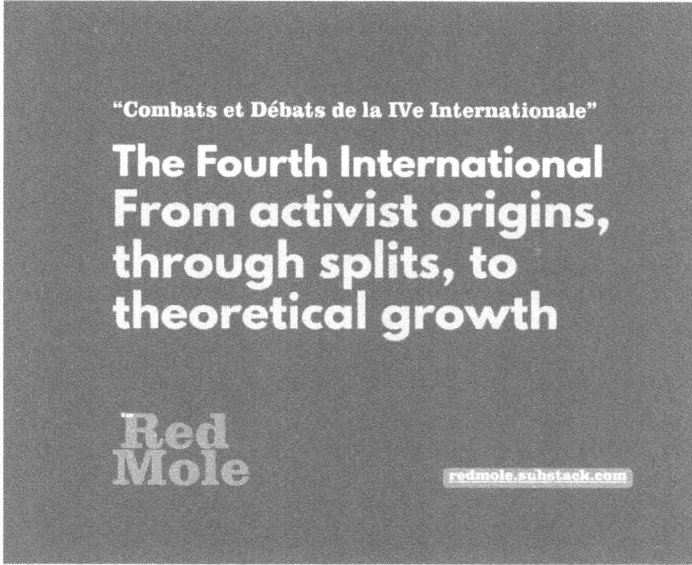

*Below is a note we previously decided not to use in [an article on splits](#)
in the Fourth International. We're sharing it because it relates to a discussion
with a reader about Pierre Moreau's book, Combats et débats de la Quatrième
Internationale.*

The Fourth International (FI), founded in 1938, emerged from the
failures of social democracy and the rise of Stalinism. Its roots trace back to the
Left Opposition formed within the Communist Party of the USSR in 1923, which
fought against the party's increasing bureaucracy and advocated for socialist
workers' democracy and a global revolutionary policy. From its start, the FI has
navigated complex revolutionary politics, beginning as an activist group rather
than an immediate mass movement. It has grown and refined its ideas through
many internal debates and divisions.

From Broad Ambition to Activist Foundation

Initially, the Fourth International aimed to unite all revolutionary groups
breaking away from both Stalinism and social democracy, not just Trotskyists.
Many non-Trotskyist organizations, some with larger memberships, were part of
this early vision. Examples included the Independent Labour Party (ILP) in Great
Britain, the Socialist Workers and Peasants Party in France, and the Workers'
Party of Marxist Unification (POUM) in Spain. The "Declaration of the Four,"
signed by the International Communist League and three left-socialist

organizations in Germany and Holland, showed that Trotskyists were willing to be a minority in a new International.

However, groups like the POUM did not join the formal establishment of the Fourth International. These parties no longer exist. The POUM, despite its importance among independent communist groups in the 1930s, failed to overcome its political isolation and internal divisions. Its indecisiveness during key moments, like the May 1937 workers' uprising in Spain, was criticized. As a result, the Fourth International was officially founded by only Trotskyists in 1938, justified by other groups' refusal to join.

At its formation, the Fourth International was numerically small, with groups from 28 countries. Most of these groups were newly formed and had only dozens of members. Despite criticisms of it being a sectarian self-proclamation, Leon Trotsky noted that the movement had waited five years before formally founding it. The debate on its foundation also highlighted the connection between building national parties and the International. Trotsky argued against different criteria for mass influence for national versus international bodies. While always aiming for mass influence, the FI began as a crucial ideological current, a "propaganda international" that had to struggle to preserve and strengthen its limited group of dedicated members.

Navigating Splits and Theoretical Revisions

The Fourth International's history has been marked by a series of significant splits and internal debates. These disagreements have, perhaps surprisingly, helped to update and refresh its theory.

One of the most significant divisions was the 1953 split, largely started by the US Socialist Workers Party (SWP). This split arose partly from disagreements over Michel Pablo's views on the transition to socialism. Critics, including the Lambertists, accused Pablo of giving too much importance to Stalinist bureaucracies, thus undermining the need for the Fourth International's independent struggle. The SWP, acting with what was described by others as "national messianism," saw itself as "the most important party in the world" and the "legitimate leader of the Trotskyist movement," resenting guidance from the International Secretariat (IS) in Paris. Cannon, the central SWP leader, famously declared that "a few people in Paris" would not dictate to the SWP. This led to the SWP's "Open Letter to Trotskyists Throughout the World" in November 1953, effectively rejecting the elected international leadership. Despite this break, the international leadership of the 1950s is credited with preventing sectarian decline and defending against tendencies that would have dissolved the movement, successfully preserving the Fourth International's organizational structure, and paving the way for reunificaiton of the public factions in 1963.

Michel Pablo's own later split in the mid-1960s was another important event. After the 1963 reunification, Pablo's changing political analysis and disagreements with the International's approach led to his departure and the formation of the Marxist Revolutionary Tendency International (TMRI). While the TMRI aimed for broader revolutionary regroupings by having members join larger parties (generalized entrism), it had limited success and eventually dissolved in 1991, with some of its members rejoining the Fourth International.

Another major internal conflict was the Morenoite split, led by Nahuel Moreno in Argentina. His group initially aligned with the SWP after the 1963 reunification, but significant political and tactical differences emerged, especially over the Portuguese Revolution (where the US SWP was particularly disoriented, and while Moreno and the FI leadership each had different parts of the needed solution) and the Angolan Civil War. This led to the breakup of the Leninist Trotskyist Faction (LTF) in 1976 and the formation of the Bolshevik Faction (BF), which increasingly acted like an "International within the International." The split of the BF and the Leninist Trotskyist Tendency (LTT) in 1979 accounted for a large minority of the International's forces, particularly in Latin America. Moreno later questioned Trotsky's theory of permanent revolution, favoring a "democratic revolution" concept instead. While his international tendency (LIT) remained primarily regional and experienced significant split from 1988, as elements like the Uruguayan section of the LIT later rejoined the Fourth International.

The US Socialist Workers Party (SWP) itself underwent a significant shift, arguably beginning in 1979 and accelerating in the 1980s. Its leadership, under Jack Barnes, openly attacked the global Trotskyist movement and rejected the theory of permanent revolution in 1983, returning to pre-1917 Leninist ideas. This resulted in purges within the SWP, leading to the formation of groups of FI members in Solidarity and the Fourth Internationalist Tendency. By the 12th World Congress in 1985, the SWP and its supporters were reduced to less than 10% of the International's membership. The SWP in Australia, initially aligned with the US SWP, also moved towards explicitly anti-Trotskyist positions.

The two parts of the IC which refused to reunify in 1963, the Healyites (Socialist Labour League in Britain) and the Lambertists (Organisation Communiste Internationaliste in France), consistently criticized the Fourth International for "Pabloism" and "revisionism." These groups diverged soon afterwards, with Healy's WRP breaking into multiple factions in 1985 and the Lambertists experiencing significant splits, ultimately moving towards dissolving into social democracy. While the Fourth International managed to preserve its organizational framework, many of the "anti-Pablist" groups often suffered further fragmentation, with many now struggling to survive.

Endurance, Growth, and Future Paths

Despite these numerous challenges and splits, the Fourth International has shown remarkable vitality and continuity. It has consistently functioned as "an international organization based on a fundamental revolutionary program and a flexible application of international democratic centralism," rejecting the idea of a "party-fraction" that characterized many rival groups. The ability to hold world congresses regularly, even during difficult times, has been crucial for its ongoing existence.

The Fourth International experienced significant expansion from 1968 to 1975, marked by the rise of a new revolutionary generation. While entrism (having members join larger parties to influence them), as seen with the "French Turn" in the 1930s, allowed Trotskyists to grow in numbers and influence, the "Italian Lesson" in the 1960s highlighted the dangers of staying too long in mass parties and missing broader waves of youth radicalization.

In the 1980s, despite a general conservative backlash and the working class being largely on the defensive in developed capitalist countries, the Fourth International maintained its membership levels in most imperialist countries. New young members compensated for losses. Its sections grew in Latin America, particularly in Mexico and Brazil, as military dictatorships faced increasing difficulties. The Mexican section, for example, became the main revolutionary, socialist, and workers' political force in the country after the dissolution of the Communist Party in 1989.

The Fourth International has consistently acknowledged its relative success compared to other revolutionary groups, such as the Maoists, whose appeal faded in the late 1970s and early 1980s. It also notes the failure of rival Trotskyist groups to establish enduring mock Internationals ("Internationales-bidon"). As Moreau argued, the Fourth International today represents "the principal framework" for those claiming to be Trotskyist, regrouping the largest number of members, national sections, and significant organizations across continents.

The Fourth International continues to seek growth and new ways to build a mass revolutionary international. These potential pathways include: breakthroughs by existing national sections into mass parties (like in Mexico); a new independent mass workers' party (such as the Brazilian Workers' Party, PT) launching a call for a new international; a convergence of revolutionary forces (for example, in Central America); or the refounding of the communist movement on new bases after the rejection of Stalinism in Eastern Europe. In all cases, the Fourth International sees itself as an active agent rather than a passive observer.

The history of the Fourth International demonstrates that its growth and decline have generally mirrored global class struggles. Its lasting contribution lies in its "uninterrupted revolutionary continuity rooted in the best period of the Communist International," a "wealth of experience in struggles across the three sectors of the world revolution," and "revolutionary activists embedded in mass movements in dozens of countries." By preserving its organizational framework and engaging in continuous theoretical self-correction through its debates and splits, the Fourth International aims to make an irreplaceable contribution to the formation of a future revolutionary international of the masses.

Contemporary Organizational Analysis

How Tommy Robinson's 150,000-Strong March Exposed the SWP's Strategic Dead End

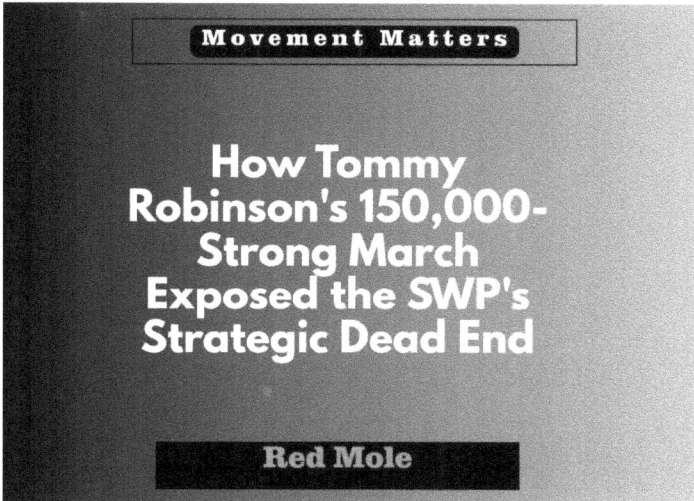

        The twenty-to-one numerical defeat at Tommy Robinson's march reveals a crisis that goes beyond numbers: the British left's fundamental inability to build the united front necessary for effective anti-fascist struggle. The "Unite the Kingdom" march on 13 September 2025, organised by far-right activist Tommy Robinson, mobilised an unprecedented 110,000 to 150,000 people, while the anti-fascist counter-protest by Stand Up to Racism drew only around 5,000 participants. This significant imbalance represents a monumental strategic defeat for the anti-fascist movement and serves as a damning indictment of its current organisational effectiveness and strategic paralysis.

        This failure was not accidental, but a direct consequence of deep-seated organisational crises, ideological confusion, and a fragmented programme. Factions from the Labour leadership to revolutionary groups offered competing and often contradictory analyses, preventing the formation of a unified and effective response. The core lesson is that the anti-fascist struggle cannot be separated from a militant, class-based programme that directly addresses the material grievances of the working class. A purely moralistic or liberal anti-racist stance proved strategically insufficient against a movement that has skilfully weaponised the anxieties of neoliberal decline.

19

1. The New Model of Far-Right Mobilisation: Creeping Fascism in a Digital Age

The mobilisation of 150,000 marchers for Tommy Robinson was not a simple replication of 1930s tactics against Oswald Mosley's British Union of Fascists or 1970s confrontations with the National Front; it represents a "new model of fascist advance" driven by fundamental changes in capitalism and technology. The question is not whether this movement is technically classical fascism (a debate often deemed futile) but rather recognising that it is part of a "fluid political process" known as "fascisation" or "creeping fascism".

This process is characterised by:

Proto-Fascist Development toward Authoritarian Democracy: Modern far-right movements do not typically organise paramilitary forces to overthrow the state by revolution, as in the interwar period. Instead, the "direction of travel of the Right as a whole" is towards an "Authoritarian Right". This aims for "authoritarian democracy" (or a managed democracy), where political life is suffocated, and democratic rights are systematically restricted, rather than eliminated outright. The essence remains counter-revolutionary: to defend the capitalist system against the threat of radical change from the working class and the oppressed.

The Digital Bypass of Traditional Organising: The march's scale was achieved by leveraging a "new, technologically enabled, and globally networked ecosystem" that "bypasses traditional organising methods". Modern fascism relies less on mass parties and Nuremberg rallies and more on a "shifting kaleidoscope of online hate channels". This online infrastructure amplifies the far-right's toxic cocktail of nationalism, racism, and misogyny, driving xenophobic narratives and inciting direct action.

The event received crucial support from international figures, notably Elon Musk, who addressed the crowd via video link with incendiary comments such as "violence is coming to you, you either fight back or you die" and a call for a "dissolution of parliament". This underscores how global capital supports this new brand of right-wing populism. The presence of foreign far-right politicians, like French politician Éric Zemmour, who spoke of a "great replacement of our European people" by migrants, further cemented the international character of the movement.

Strategic Imperative: The response cannot be based on fighting "the last war". While the primary agent of fascist repression remains the existing bourgeois state, the far right provides the ideology and the "auxiliaries". Revolutionary Marxists must fight the real tendency of the bourgeoisie towards the "strong state" through persistent daily battles, while opposing the potentially catastrophic danger of open fascism.

2. Organisational Mapping: The Crisis of the United Front

The left's "monumental strategic defeat" was fundamentally a "consequence of a profound inability to build a united front capable of mass mobilisation". The fragmentation of the response, particularly concerning SUTR's strategy, demands a sharp organisational critique based on Leninist united front logic.

THE SUTR FAILURE: FROM GENUINE FRONT TO PARTY FRONT

The model employed by SUTR/SWP suffered from three key strategic weaknesses:

Lack of Democratic and Class-Based Culture: While SUTR/SWP was the central actor in the counter-protest, the mobilisation was undermined by a lack of clear political direction and a refusal to adopt a clear, "working-class, anti-austerity programme". The anti-fascist struggle "cannot be separated from a militant, class-based programme". True unity of action against fascism requires exposing the failures of the far-right by addressing the material grievances exploited by nationalist demagogy, such as the "real insecurities of working-class communities around shortages of housing, jobs, and services".

Sectarian Isolation vs. Coalition: The united front principle demands "March separately, but strike together!" The revolutionary party must maintain "complete freedom of criticism of temporary allies" while seeking "agreements for mass action". The failure of SUTR to function as a genuine united front, incorporating other forces effectively, contrasts starkly with historical successes:

Cable Street Model: The 1936 victory was achieved by a genuine united front, including local activists, trade unionists, and community groups. Critically, while the Communist Party claimed credit in semi-official histories, it was actually the ILP and sections of the Labour Party who were the backbone of the mobilisation, focusing on working-class unity rather than the CPGB's "Popular Front" with bourgeois interests. The strength of the mobilisation was in spite of CPGB politics rather than because of it.

The Critique of "Smashism" (Elitist Tactics): The defeat highlights the necessity of avoiding small-group confrontations in favour of mass action. "Smashism" has been associated with elitist tactics, such as Red Action-dominated AFA branches, which operate as an "elitist hit squad" seeking to "trash the fash". This approach must be rejected in favour of strategies traditional to the workers' movement—namely, mass pickets and mass action designed to overwhelm and disperse the opponent, as used at Cable Street.

THE NEED FOR GEOGRAPHIC DIFFERENTIATION

The strategic response must be flexible, recognising that "one size doesn't fit all" for anti-fascist organising, as the struggle must be based on a "precise appraisal of the specific historical situation and, primarily, of economic conditions".

The Scottish Dynamic: The existence of a strong "left-liberal bourgeois force" like the Scottish National Party creates a different political context for far-right advance compared to England. While the SNP remains a bourgeois nationalist force, it may temporarily alter the dynamics of the struggle by providing an alternative to traditional British ruling class parties. Furthermore, Reform UK's approach in Scotland notably drops their central focus on independence to concentrate explicitly on austerity and anti-migrant themes, requiring revolutionaries to adapt tactics accordingly.

3. Synthesis of Action: Balancing Mass Mobilisation with Community Organising

The strategic defeat on September 13th was rooted in the failure to leverage the full, organised power of the working class. To overcome this, the anti-fascist struggle must adopt a "combination and synthesis" of mass mobilisation tactics and bottom-up community organising.

Mass Action as the Essential Aim

While grassroots work is indispensable, mass mobilisation remains the "essential aim" of anti-fascist organising, primarily by blocking the far right's major propaganda functions—their marches, meetings, and demonstrations. The objective in imperialist countries is the "unification of the proletarian forces" on an anti-capitalist basis.

The Grassroots Foundation and Self-Defence

Mass mobilisation cannot succeed without strong forms of "self-organisation" built from the bottom up. The working class needs organised self-activity. This strategy must emphasise the creation of community-based self-defence networks to protect vulnerable communities. These measures are part of preparing the movement for inevitable confrontation while maintaining the focus on mass political work and mass intimidation, not "Smashism" or elitist tactics.

The trade union movement, with its 6.5 million members, failed to mobilise its full strength, a tactical failure that played a significant role in the defeat. The trade union movement must be a central pillar of any future anti-fascist organising, providing not only banners but also the resources, organising capacity, and authority needed for a successful mass campaign.

4. Strengthening the Starmer Government Analysis: Bourgeois Enablement

The response of the Labour leadership—what can be categorised as the "Conservative Left" approach—must be framed as a specific strategic failure that objectively functions as bourgeois enablement of the far right.

Labour's Strategic Failure and Normalisation

The "Conservative Left" strategy views the far right primarily as a threat to liberal institutions, emphasising legal and political containment. This approach fails strategically because it refuses ideological confrontation.

Normalisation: Labour leaders normalise the far right's mobilisation by framing it within the bounds of liberal tolerance. The Business Secretary's defence of the large turnout as proof that "free speech, free association, is alive and well" exemplifies how the political establishment seeks to neutralise the threat by treating it as a legitimate democratic expression, rather than an accelerating proto-fascist development.

Failure to Address Material Grievances: The Labour leadership avoids a militant, class-based programme. The failure to address the underlying "social and economic misery of neoliberal austerity" and the "real insecurities of working-class communities" means the political ground exploited by the far right remains unchallenged and fertile.

Social Democracy as an Objective Obstacle

This strategic failure conforms to a historical pattern where the moderate wing of the workers' movement acts as an "objective obstacle" to anti-fascist victory. When faced with crisis, the bankruptcy of moderate politics "drives the despairing petty bourgeois into the arms of the fascists". The Labour Party's strategic impotence and illusions in parliamentary democracy ensures that the capitalist ruling class, which regards the fascist gangs as useful "auxiliaries", can maintain its power.

5. Contemporary Digital Strategy: Countering Post-Truth Disinfotainment

The modern far-right threat is intrinsically linked to its technological model, requiring a comprehensive "sophisticated digital strategy" as a central pillar of the Revolutionary Democracy response.

The Networked Threat and Weaponised Disinformation

The march's success was enabled by a "new, technologically enabled, and globally networked ecosystem". This operates as a "shifting kaleidoscope of online hate channels" that accelerate radicalisation through "disaster disinfotainment"—manufactured narratives exploiting global crises to activate "vengeful passions against well-selected enemies".

The "Post-Truth" Dynamic: This disinformation thrives on a lack of trust in traditional authority. In an environment where neoliberalism fosters competition and distrust, people turn toward "DIY investigation" because they cannot trust established sources. There's a critical point where people stop caring whether what they think is true or not—this erosion of rational judgment is exactly what revolutionaries must address.

The Revolutionary Counter-Strategy

The left cannot simply dismiss the "culture war" and focus only on economics; this would risk siding with forces attacking the oppressed. The digital strategy must target the "capacities of rational judgement of interests, of ends and means" to counter the far-right's reliance on irrationalism. This must be paired with mass campaigning that exposes the links between the far right, global capital, and the political establishment while offering a clear vision for an alternative, socialist future.

6. Immediate Strategic Lessons for Today's Organisers

The Centrality of Class Struggle: The far-right's advance is fuelled by the social and economic misery of neoliberal austerity, skilfully channelling legitimate anger into xenophobic demagogy. The left must stop viewing immigration as a "legitimate concern" to be managed and instead fight for a clear, anti-austerity, class-based programme. A moralistic opposition to racism must be combined with firm economic demands for jobs, homes, services, and protection of living standards to cut the ground from beneath the far-right's narrative of national decline.

The Imperative of a United Front: The most critical lesson is the imperative to overcome the left's deep-seated sectarian fragmentation. This requires "practical cooperation in a non-sectarian way" with other left parties and movements while maintaining "complete freedom of criticism of temporary allies". The aim is to unite various forces in action, not to merge programmes or banners.

A Forward-Looking Strategy: The new, transnational, and digitally-enabled nature of the far right demands a similarly sophisticated response. This includes building community-based self-defence networks, launching mass campaigns that expose far-right links to global capital, and developing comprehensive digital counter-strategies.

The meaning of September 13 is not that the fascists have won, but that the left has been given a wake-up call to reorganise and fight back on new terms. By embracing a strategy rooted in a militant, class-based programme and a unified front, the left can transform this strategic defeat into a catalyst for a new, more effective revolutionary movement. The response cannot be based on fighting the last war—it must address the contemporary reality of creeping fascism in the digital age while drawing on the proven principles of working-class solidarity and mass action.

FURTHER READING

Here are recommended items for further reading:

Fascism: How to Smash It: This document, produced by the International Marxist Group, is extensively cited for its insights into the nature of fascism, its exploitation of racism within the working class, and the complex role of the bourgeoisie in simultaneously deploring and enabling far-right movements. It offers crucial historical and strategic lessons on street-based anti-fascist tactics and the importance of a united front.

Leon Trotsky, The Struggle Against Fascism in Germany: This work by Leon Trotsky, with an introduction by Ernest Mandel, is a foundational Marxist text for understanding fascism's rise and how to combat it. It provides detailed analysis of the united front tactic, critiques of sectarianism (such as "social fascism"), and lessons from the German experience, which are directly relevant to contemporary anti-fascist strategy.

"IMG 1975 Internal Discussion Bulletin Struggle Against Racism and Fascism": This internal discussion bulletin from the International Marxist Group (IMG) offers historical context on the IMG's anti-racist and anti-fascist work. It provides a detailed analysis of racism as an ideology of imperialism, its reflection within the labour movement, and the tactical challenges of combating it, including the exploitation of "backward traditions" among workers.

"Creeping Fascism Revisited": Faulkner's Creeping Fascism Revisited is essential reading. These insights provided contemporary analysis of the far right, including its evolution, the concept of "creeping fascism," and the bourgeoisie's role. They also discuss the nature of modern authoritarianism and different strategic approaches to combating it, such as popular frontism.

"Excavating Hope among the Ruins: Confronting Creeping Fascism in Our Midst" This source provides a contemporary analysis of "creeping fascism" and its characteristics.

Why the CWI failed to back the Irish left's landslide victory

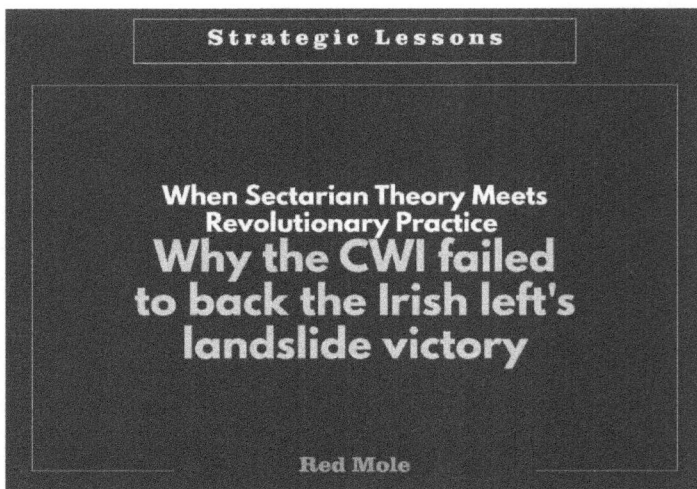

In October 2025, Ireland's revolutionary left faced a decisive test. Catherine Connolly, backed by a united left coalition including People Before Profit, the Social Democrats, Labour, Greens, and Sinn Féin, won the presidential election with a historic landslide. She secured the largest percentage and largest total vote of any presidential candidate in Irish history. For the first time in the state's history, the left won a majority of votes in a national election. Young voters swung decisively leftward; 57% of 18-34 year olds voted for Connolly compared to just 17% for the establishment candidate. Thousands of new activists were mobilised, momentum was regained by the left, and a concrete foundation was laid for building toward a left government.

Yet not all of the Irish left participated in this historic victory. Militant Left, the Irish section of the Committee for a Workers' International (CWI), stood aside. They argued that joining a "coalition of the left" with Labour and Greens meant compromising with capitalist parties; therefore, revolutionaries must maintain sectarian purity and abstain from participation. The result was that Militant Left isolated itself from the historic opening while the left won decisively.

Militant Left's error is not isolated. The same sectarian logic is increasingly evident across the international left. In Italy, the Revolutionary Communist International (RCI), a split from the same Committee for a Workers' International, has adopted identical ultra-left tactics, organising a provocation against feminist organisations. Their practice mirrors Militant Left's isolation; refusing to photograph other revolutionary organisations' banners, editorialising other groups out of struggles, and substituting abstract purity for participation in

26

mass movements.

Most significantly, this sectarian approach has moved beyond mere organisational practice into theoretical justification. The article "Lenin's Method for Revolutionary Party Building" (Il metodo di Lenin nella costruzione del partito rivoluzionario) by Concetto Solano provides precisely such a justification. Recently cited in the Tendency for a Revolutionary International Facebook group, Solano's framework mechanically privileges internal purity over strategic engagement, arguing that the party "can't and shouldn't adapt to labour spontaneity" because it is "permeated by the influence of the ruling class". This theoretical argument provides intellectual cover for the very sectarian practice that Militant Left and the RCI are pursuing.

The Irish presidential election provides a crucial test case for these competing approaches. The results demonstrate concretely what the abstract debate obscures: Solano's framework, applied in real organisational conditions, produces isolation and irrelevance. Strategic engagement combined with programmatic clarity produces revolutionary effectiveness and growth.

The Theoretical Framework: Understanding Solano's Argument

The article "Lenin's Method for Revolutionary Party Building" correctly highlights several fundamental aspects of Leninist thought, such as the imperative of organising revolutionary militants around the communist programme, and affirming that the party must not be replaced by a mere "syndicate". We also share the conclusion that the early Communist International consciously campaigned against "workerism" (economism or syndicalism), emphasising that the movement must proceed beyond purely economic struggles to a political challenge for power.

However, by mechanically focusing on the principle that the party "can't and shouldn't adapt to labour spontaneity" because it is "permeated by the influence of the ruling class", the article risks presenting a dangerously one-sided account of Lenin's method. This interpretation leads to an abstract strategic position that, in practice, risks substituting sectarian isolation for revolutionary strategy.

Lenin's Dialectical Method, Not Mechanical Purity

The assertion that the party "can't and shouldn't adapt to the labour spontaneity" is abstract and overlooks Lenin's strategic instruction, which demands the constant necessity of utilising all available means to connect with the masses. Lenin was not advocating for sectarian withdrawal from movements deemed "impure"; he was insisting on strategic engagement combined with ideological clarity.

Strategy Built on Mass Movement: Revolutionary strategy must always be built upon "the movement of the masses". While the early Marxist tenet (as cited in the article) that class political consciousness must be brought to the workers "only from without" holds true, the masses are ultimately won over "only by action". The spontaneous upsurge of the working class is acknowledged in Lenin's tradition as the essential raw material and the "embryonic form of organisation". Mechanically rejecting spontaneity risks misunderstanding the very dialectical process required for the revolutionary party to conquer the majority of the working class.

The Necessity of Penetration, Not Purity: Ideological clarity is vital, but Lenin's practical method prioritised penetration over purity to avoid ultra-left isolation. When struggling within mass bodies such as trade unions, Lenin urged revolutionaries to exercise patience, accept necessary compromises, and employ flexible tactics to achieve revolutionary aims. This flexibility, which permits participation in struggles that might initially appear reformist or "impure," is crucial for linking immediate victories to the ultimate goal of working-class power.

The Party as the Tribune of the People

Solano correctly stresses the indispensable role of the theoretically aware vanguard. However, the notion that the party only becomes an "indispensable tool" when the working class acquires "awareness of its historical role" is misleading.

The Leninist party must operate actively in the present moment, championing not merely its internal rigour but acting as the "tribune of the people" This requires the party to champion "every manifestation of tyranny and oppression" regardless of the stratum or class it affects. This comprehensive mandate extends to supporting all progressive democratic struggles and constantly emphasising the need to link the fight against capitalism with the "fight for the widest democracy". The party must pursue this comprehensive democratic approach to clarify the "world-historic significance of the struggle for the emancipation of the proletariat". By narrowly focusing on the party's internal self-consciousness and abstractly condemning spontaneity, Solano's framework misses this broad, interventionist mandate.

The Sectarian Approach in Practice: Militant Left's Fatal Error

What does Solano's logic produce when applied to actual revolutionary work? The answer is visible in Ireland. Militant Left's position directly mirrored Solano's theoretical framework: the party "cannot and shouldn't adapt" to such combinations with Labour and Greens because these parties are "permeated by the influence of the ruling class," and therefore principled revolutionaries must stand aside in the name of purity. The result was that Militant Left isolated itself from the historic opening while the left won decisively.

This was not a marginal decision. The Connolly campaign mobilised hundreds of thousands of workers, young people, and activists into electoral struggle. It created the conditions for revolutionary organisations to demonstrate effectiveness on a mass scale, to win new layers to advanced political positions, and to build concrete organisational capacity. Militant Left's sectarian abstention meant standing aside precisely when revolutionary work was most fertile.

The Strategic Approach in Practice: People Before Profit's Vindication

People Before Profit (which includes the Fourth International permanent observer, RISE) adopted the opposite approach. Rather than retreating into sectarian purity, they actively participated in the Connelly campaign, using it to build momentum for a left government, win new activists, and establish the precedent of left unity. Crucially, they maintained complete ideological and organisational independence throughout. As Paul Murphy (a PBP parliamentarian) explained, their condition for participation was unambiguous: "we retain our right to independence, to put forward our own ecosocialist position, and continue strengthening our connections with communities to mobilise the power of people from below."

This is precisely what Lenin meant by the United Front tactic. It is not about endorsing reformist politics; it is about participating in common struggle to win the masses to revolutionary conclusions.

Catherine Connolly's victory bore out this approach. She won with the largest vote share in Irish presidential history; this was not a close result but a definitive popular mandate. The demographic breakdown tells the story of what became possible through participation:

- 57% of 18-34 year olds voted for Connolly; only 17% voted for the establishment candidate Heather Humphreys
- Among 35-54 year olds, Connolly polled 49%
- The Irish Times interviewed 35 first-time voters; 29 were voting for Connolly, 5 were spoiling their ballot, and only 1 was voting for Humphreys
- Thousands of new activists were mobilised for the first time and gained organising experience

Momentum that had slipped rightward was regained by the left

A concrete foundation was laid for building toward a left government.

As Paul Murphy wrote in the aftermath, directly addressing the sectarian tendency: "Those sections of the socialist left who gave grudging endorsements for Catherine while criticising PBP's engagement in the campaign will hopefully reflect on what happened and what they stood aside from. A left-right polarisation took place, and the left won."

The Catherine Connolly victory demonstrates what Solano's framework obscures: the relationship between revolutionary organisation and mass struggle is not one of external judgment and moral condemnation, but of dialectical engagement and strategic participation. Consider what actually occurred:

Revolutionary organisation did not weaken itself through participation: PBP maintained complete ideological and organisational independence throughout the campaign. As Murphy noted, their condition for participation was simple: "we retain our right to independence, to put forward our own ecosocialist position, and continue strengthening our connections with communities to mobilise the power of people from below." They did not dissolve into the reformist parties; they used the campaign to strengthen themselves.

Tactical flexibility enabled strategic victory: By participating in the broad Connolly coalition, revolutionaries were able to demonstrate through action that they were "the most resolute and effective fighters." They built trust with other left formations, with mass movements, and crucially, with tens of thousands of previously non-political people. This is precisely what Lenin meant by the United Front tactic; it is not about endorsing reformist politics, but about participating in common struggle to win the masses to revolutionary conclusions.

The party's tribune role was enlarged, not diminished: By championing Connolly's anti-imperialist programme, her defence of Palestinian liberation, her opposition to NATO rearmament, and her housing justice demands, revolutionary socialists demonstrated that they could be the "tribune of the people" on all questions affecting the masses, not just narrow "class" issues. This is what enabled revolutionary forces to gain hearing among 57% of young voters.

Sectarian purity guaranteed marginality: Militant Left's stance meant that when a historic opening developed, when the masses were ready to engage in electoral struggle around left demands, revolutionaries stood aside preaching abstract purity. The concrete result: marginalisation and irrelevance while history moved on without them.

The Dialectics of Spontaneity and Consciousness Revisited

Solano writes that the party "can't and shouldn't adapt to labour spontaneity" because it is "permeated by the influence of the ruling class." This is true in the abstract; ruling-class ideology does permeate spontaneous struggle. But this is precisely why the party must engage with spontaneity, not withdraw from it. The dialectical process of raising consciousness requires the meeting point between revolutionary theory and spontaneous practice.

In Ireland in October 2025, hundreds of thousands of workers, young people, and activists moved into struggle motivated by economic demands (housing), anti-imperialist solidarity (Gaza), and democratic aspirations (neutrality and opposition to rearmament). Their consciousness was shaped by ruling-class ideology; they initially saw a presidential campaign, not a revolutionary transformation. And yet, by participating alongside them while maintaining ideological clarity and organisational independence, revolutionaries were able to deepen that struggle, win new layers to advanced positions, and build organisational capacity.

The Connolly victory proved that Lenin's method is not about mechanical rejection of "impure" struggle. It is about strategic engagement: entering into every struggle the masses undertake, learning alongside them, demonstrating revolutionary effectiveness through action, and patiently linking immediate demands to the ultimate goal of workers' power.

Avoiding Ultra-Left Isolation

The strategy recommended by Lenin requires combining "enthusiasm and cold calculation", ensuring a "firm political identity" while consciously avoiding the dogmatism that leads to isolation. The fundamental strategic error inherent in rejecting engagement with spontaneity is that it hinders the crucial work of revolutionary strategy: patiently entering every struggle, no matter how small or "impure," to link immediate victories to the ultimate goal of working-class power.

This practice mirrors the errors Lenin attacked in Left-Wing Communism: An Infantile Disorder; groups that refused to work in mass organisations, that abstained from electoral struggles, that stood aside from spontaneous movements in the name of revolutionary purity. They believed they were protecting their organisations from corruption. In practice, they guaranteed their own irrelevance.

A revolutionary organisation committed to Leninist strategy cannot build strategy "upon the possibility of an exceptional, easy victory", but must patiently engage in tactical work to win the majority of the working class. The Catherine Connolly campaign showed what this looks like in practice: thousands of new activists, tens of thousands of votes, demonstrated revolutionary effectiveness, strengthened organisational capacity, and a concrete foundation for building toward a left government.

Conclusion: From Theory to Practice, From Isolation to Irrelevance

The crisis revealed in Ireland is symptomatic of a broader malaise affecting sections of the international left. When organisations like Militant Left, the RCI, and others adopt Solano's theoretical framework, they set themselves on a path toward sectarian isolation. When they refuse to participate in mass struggles because those struggles are "permeated by ruling-class ideology," they guarantee their own irrelevance.

This is not an argument for abandoning revolutionary independence or programme. Rather, it is an insistence that revolutionary independence is maintained and sharpened through engagement with struggle, not through withdrawal from it. It is an insistence that Leninist method is dialectical; it engages with the actual movement of the masses as it exists, even when that movement is shaped by ruling-class ideology and reformist politics. Through that engagement, combined with ideological clarity and organisational coherence, consciousness is raised and revolutionary capacity is built.

The Catherine Connolly victory proves the living power of genuine Leninist strategy. It also provides a cautionary tale for those who would substitute abstract principles of purity for the hard work of revolutionary engagement with the masses. History moves on; the only question is whether revolutionary organisation will participate in shaping it or stand aside preaching doctrine to empty rooms.

The choice before the international left is clear. Embrace the dialectical method that Lenin actually practiced, or follow Solano's mechanical framework into increasing isolation. The Irish people have already made their choice. They demonstrated that when the left unites around a genuinely progressive programme and shows revolutionary effectiveness through action, the masses respond decisively. The question is whether revolutionary organisations will learn that lesson before sectarian purity consumes them entirely.

Zarah Sultana and the Politics of Left Distinction

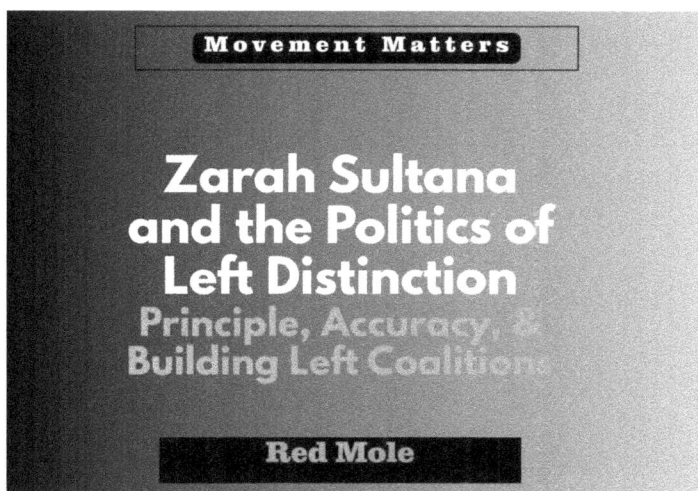

Zarah Sultana MP's stance on NATO has become both clearer and more uncompromising in recent weeks. Her October 28 X post calling NATO an "imperialist war machine" and arguing for Britain's immediate withdrawal leaves little room for ambiguity. She pointed to NATO's roles in Afghanistan and Libya not as isolated blunders but as evidence of systemic dysfunction. She also linked rising military spending to collapsing public services: "Arms dealers profit while our NHS collapses, public services crumble and millions of children grow up in poverty." Here Sultana ties anti-imperialist politics directly to working-class interests and broader anti-capitalist criticism.

Within Your Party, there is broad support for this NATO stance, though opinions on sending weapons to Ukraine remain divided.

The Your Party Differentiation: Factual Problems

Sultana's PoliticsJOE interview attempted to set Your Party apart from the Greens, especially on foreign policy. She claimed Your Party rejects diplomatic ties with Israel, unlike the Greens—a comment that provoked immediate pushback. Phil Proudfoot noted the Greens have voted to classify the Israeli military as a terrorist group, back BDS, and support arms embargoes. Owen Jones added that the Greens favor proscribing the IDF and pursue class-based politics.

More fundamentally, both the Scottish Green Party and the Green Party of England and Wales have platforms that go further than Sultana suggested. The Scottish Greens openly describe Zionism as a racist, supremacist ideology, support BDS, and define the Israeli-Palestinian conflict as settler colonialism. The GPEW labels Israel's claim to be a "Jewish state" as racist, calls its actions apartheid and genocide, and condemns Zionism. Both advocate ending arms exports to Israel and cutting diplomatic ties.

Sultana's depiction of the Greens as too soft on Israel therefore misrepresents parties with even stronger anti-Zionist positions than those she articulates. As Julian Atkinson observed, using supposed ambiguities as an excuse to avoid collaboration is simply sectarianism—but when the "ambiguities" are factual errors about parties holding stronger anti-Zionist positions, the sectarianism becomes particularly acute.

The Pattern of Inaccuracy

At a Your Party event in Glasgow, Sultana incorrectly claimed the Scottish Greens don't oppose Zionism, overlooking their explicit support for BDS and criticism of Zionism as racist. Mark Ballard, a Scottish Green, clarified that both Green parties oppose NATO membership, countering any suggestion that they and Your Party differ fundamentally on this issue.

This pattern raises a real challenge for groups like Your Party: Is their anti-imperialist stance grounded in principle or in drawing lines between themselves and others? If the former, then getting facts right about other left groups is essential for credibility. Establishing distinct identity should rest on genuine policy differences, not misstating other parties' positions. If Sultana and Your Party leaders aren't accurate about the Greens, it undermines their broader authority.

Assessment: Credibility and Scrupulousness

Anti-imperialist politics carry real weight when paired with intellectual honesty. Sultana's opposition to NATO and the Israeli government is clear and principled, but credibility suffers when other organizations are mischaracterized. For the Scottish left, making progress depends on open dialogue and honest debate, not factional point-scoring.

Whether Your Party can balance firm, principled positions with careful, accurate analysis will be crucial for building left unity. The stakes are significant: genuine strategic opportunities exist for radical politics in Scotland, but they can only be seized through scrupulous engagement with other left organizations, not through the repeated mischaracterization of their actual positions.

Beyond Sectarian Framings: The Ukraine Question and United Front Strategy

Sultana's opposition to arms shipments to Ukraine from NATO members represents a genuine disagreement within anti-imperialist circles, not a position equivalent to supporting Russia or Putin. This distinction matters strategically. Sultana explicitly opposes the Russian invasion and condemns Putin's dictatorship. Her critique of NATO arms provision rests on the argument that Western military aid subordinates Ukraine to imperialist conditionalities and Western strategic interests rather than serving Ukrainian liberation.

This disagreement is real and substantive, but framing those who hold it as "supporters of Putin" or surrogates of the Kremlin is both factually inaccurate and strategically counterproductive. Such framings prevent the common action that remains possible on genuine shared ground. The left cannot build effective united fronts by excluding everyone who disagrees on specific tactical questions about arms transfers while agreeing on opposition to Russian invasion, support for Ukrainian self-determination, and the need to defend Ukrainian workers and social movements.

The more productive strategic question is: On what concrete demands can we organize together? Justine Brabant's framework, outlined in her Mediapart article "La guerre russe contre l'Ukraine: Un autre soutien à l'Ukraine était possible," points toward unifying demands that transcend the arms provision debate. These include debt cancellation for Ukraine, protection of Ukrainian labour rights against imposed neoliberal reforms, use of frozen Russian assets and expropriation of oligarchs to fund reconstruction, energy transition away from Russian fossil fuels, accountability for war crimes, and direct solidarity with Ukrainian trade unions and social movements.

These demands offer multiple entry points for organizations and activists who oppose NATO arms provision. Someone opposed to Western military aid can nonetheless advocate for:

- Immediate cancellation of Ukraine's debt, rejecting the burden of loans disguised as aid
- Protection and expansion of Ukrainian workers' rights against neoliberal "reforms" imposed alongside Western aid
- Expropriation of Ukrainian and Russian oligarchs to fund reconstruction and social provision
- Energy independence through transition to renewables, reducing reliance on both Russian and Western corporate interests
- Direct "from below" solidarity with Ukrainian grassroots organizations, trade unions, and feminist movements
- Transparency and accountability in how aid is distributed and military spending is used

These are not secondary or decorative demands. They address core questions of Ukrainian national liberation: whether Ukraine can defend itself while maintaining political independence from imperialist subordination; whether reconstruction serves ordinary Ukrainians or corporate interests; whether the war's conclusion will bring genuine self-determination or imposed division.

For the left to be effective, the strategic choice is clear: Do we organize with people who agree with us on everything except NATO arms provision, focusing on the concrete positive demands we do share? Or do we spend energy excluding them as Kremlin surrogates, thereby fragmenting the left and abandoning potential allies on the very demands that could build broader movements?

This is not about defending or excusing positions we disagree with.

Sultana and others may be wrong about the necessity of certain weapons transfers for Ukrainian defence. But being wrong about tactics for supporting Ukraine is not the same as supporting Russia. The left's historical weakness in building united fronts often stems from treating tactical disagreements as character questions or loyalty tests, thereby fragmenting potential allies over specifics while ignoring common ground on fundamentals.

A mature left politics would acknowledge: We disagree on NATO arms provision. Here are the arguments on both sides. But we can build campaigns together on debt cancellation, workers' rights protection, oligarch expropriation, and direct aid to Ukrainian grassroots movements. These demands serve Ukrainian liberation while remaining consistent with anti-imperialist principle.

Intellectual Retreat vs. Sectarian Bunkers: How the German Left Responds to Crisis

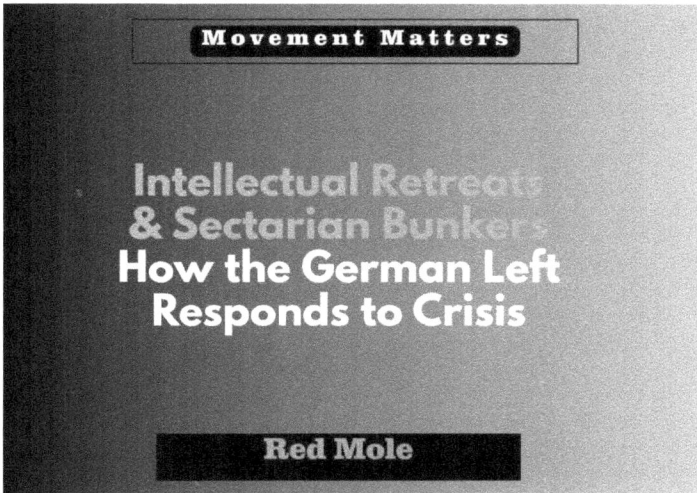

When the Alternative for Germany (AfD) achieved historic electoral breakthroughs across eastern German states in 2024-2025, it posed a stark question to the international left: how do we respond when fascists are winning? The German left's divergent responses—from Die Linke's principled recovery to BSW's nationalist retreat—offer a crucial case study in the strategic choices facing socialist movements worldwide.

This fascist surge created a moment of truth for Germany's left, revealing fundamental strategic divergences that mirror global patterns. Faced with crisis, does the left retreat intellectually by accommodating far-right narratives, isolate itself in "sectarian bunkers" of ideological purity, or successfully build a principled alternative? For international socialist organisations, this moment is not just a German problem but a crucial case study for the global class struggle.

The AfD's Ascent and the Crisis for the Left

The AfD is no ordinary conservative party; it is a stramm rechte, nationalistische und rassistische Partei (firmly right-wing, nationalist, and racist party), with its officially dissolved but still dominant fascist wing, "Der Flügel," controlling the federal association. Their ideology is built on propaganda against non-Germans, especially refugees, and opposition to societal liberalisation since the late 1960s.

They advocate for a "Germany first" policy, rejection of the European Union in favour of a "Europe of fatherlands," and increased militarisation, while simultaneously critiquing government health, climate, and education policies. The AfD's strategy weaponises non-specific fears among middle and lower-middle classes about economic decline, presenting uncontrolled immigration as the primary cause.

They frame the political struggle as "us inside" versus "them outside," advocating for an authoritarian state to enforce a "healthy popular will". This rhetoric has resonated deeply, particularly in eastern Germany, where resentment over perceived historical marginalisation remains strong.

The party's ability to drive official government policy on refugee issues stems from other mainstream parties (excluding Die Linke) also holding racist positions, albeit less openly, thereby normalising openly racist and fascist ideas within the "bourgeois centre". This rise is a symptom of decades of crisis within neoliberal democracies and their institutions, marked by growing inequalities and governments' failure to meet people's needs.

Die Linke's Resurgence: A Principled Stand

This fascist surge created a moment of truth for Germany's left, revealing fundamental strategic divergences that would soon appear across European socialist movements. In the face of this aggressive rightward lurch, Die Linke has shown a remarkable, if challenging, recovery.

After a period of stagnation, the party underwent an "existential debate" culminating in the departure of Sahra Wagenknecht in autumn 2023. Many long-standing activists saw this departure as an opportunity to fight for Die Linke, now that Wagenknecht and her "racist politics" were gone. This internal realignment was fundamental in building resistance.

Following this, Die Linke launched a participatory offensive, focusing on strengthening local structures and aligning its program with the main concerns of the people. Their slogan, "everyone wants to govern, we want change," underscored a class-political approach, emphasising building power from below.

This strategy attracted a significant influx of 60,000 new members within four months, effectively marking a "re-foundation" of the party. Many new members were drawn to the idea of doing politics differently, anchoring themselves in neighbourhoods and working with people, rather than for them.

Lessons for today's activists: This approach demonstrates the power of concrete, grassroots engagement. Campaigns exemplified this, such as the "heating costs campaign," where Die Linke helped tenants claim back 15% of incorrectly billed heating costs, directly impacting people's lives and building trust at the local level. The party now plans to continue such extra-parliamentary work, pushing for radical reforms like rent caps or municipalisation through organising tenants and mass mobilisations.

Crucially, Die Linke's recovery was strongly linked to its clear and unwavering stance against fascism. During the federal election campaign, while other parties incited hatred against refugees, Die Linke stood as a consistent anti-fascist force, attracting those protesting against the far-right. This principled position was vital for its acceptance and ability to become a focal point for anti-fascist coalitions, including radical climate groups.

Internally, there's a growing consensus for a "socialism from below" model, advocating for term limits and salary caps for parliamentarians to prevent drifting into parliamentary politics. This represents a conscious effort to challenge the "parliamentary illusion" that often plagues left parties.

However, the party still faces challenges, particularly in strengthening its foothold in workplaces and engaging with key class conflicts beyond union officials. On the issue of Palestine, while some MPs and party leaders have shifted towards a clearer stance, the party has had a contradictory approach, navigating reputational concerns and internal debates.

The BSW's Path: A Retreat into "Left-Conservatism"

In stark contrast to Die Linke's principled recovery, the formation of Sahra Wagenknecht's new party, Bündnis Sahra Wagenknecht (BSW), in 2023 represents what we can identify as a classic case of "intellectual retreat" under pressure.

Wagenknecht, a former parliamentary leader of Die Linke, distinguished herself with a populist and nationalist discourse, particularly concerning immigration, and expressed scepticism regarding climate change. Her movement, designed "literally in her image and likeness," openly aimed to compete for votes with the AfD, often using similar arguments on asylum issues.

The BSW's platform exemplifies intellectual retreat: it is characterised as "left-conservative," advocating for Marktwirtschaft (market economy), Leistungsgesellschaft (performance-based society), national limits on politics, regulation of immigration, and opposition to "quota and gender craze" and "exaggerated climate protection".

This approach represents plundering theoretical concepts from bourgeois proponents of the "social market economy," right-wing social democracy, and even the new right's nationalistic rhetoric. Rather than maintaining a clear anti-capitalist analysis, BSW attempts to "reinvent anti-capitalism in the shadow of a new conservatism".

By focusing on "national workers" and seeking alliances with employers against immigrant workers, BSW's approach divides the working class and distances itself from class struggle principles. This "capitulation" makes the left indistinguishable from neoliberal parties and inadvertently strengthens racist sentiments, ultimately serving the far-right's interests by normalising their positions.

Strategic insight: While BSW achieved impressive electoral results in 2024 regional elections, its success represents a dangerous precedent. The party's focus on "peace" is critiqued as moralistic rather than materialist, failing to identify war as a result of capitalist production relations. The BSW is seen not as a transitional stage to a new left mass party, but as a path towards further theoretical superficiality and political adaptation to the right.

The Sectarian Bunker Alternative: Learning from Fragmentation

The German experience illuminates three distinct pathways that appear across international socialist movements. Beyond intellectual retreat, the left also faces the trap of sectarian isolation—what we might call the "bunker" response to crisis.

While Germany's main split occurred between Die Linke and BSW, the broader European left demonstrates this sectarian pattern more clearly. Similar fragmentation patterns emerge across Europe, from France's NPA splits between "open" and "closed" models to Britain's persistent revolutionary left fragmentation.

The #ZeroCovid campaign in Germany offers one example of well-intentioned sectarianism. Though initially successful in gathering signatures, the campaign was critiqued for its narrow focus on a single measure (lockdown to zero infections). This approach generated controversy rather than broad mobilisation, ultimately failing to unite the left around a comprehensive pandemic response that connected health, economic, and social justice concerns.

What characterises sectarian bunkers:

- Ideological purism over practical engagement: Prioritising theoretical correctness over building mass movements
- Fragmentation rather than unity: The "great political and ideological fragmentation of the social movements and the Left" stems from geopolitical upheavals, technological change, and intensified neoliberal individualism
- "Purist forms of horizontalism" that reject necessary organisational structures
- Factionalism and infighting across leftwing organisations that waste energy on internal conflicts rather than building external power

Historical lessons from Comintern defeats, such as the German Revolution of 1923, underscore the crucial importance of a united front and effective leadership to bridge immediate struggles and the fight for power. The failure to build such unity allows right-wing populists to offer "simple" solutions in times of crisis.

Building Principled Alternatives: Lessons for International Movements

The German case illuminates a third path beyond intellectual retreat and sectarian bunkers: principled alternative-building. Die Linke's recovery demonstrates that unwavering principles, rather than compromise or isolation, are fundamental in building effective resistance.

This approach, advocated by international socialist organisations, involves several key elements that activists worldwide can apply:
1. Boldly reaffirming anti-capitalist and internationalist principles This means unwavering opposition to imperialism from all sides and concrete

solidarity with the oppressed. Die Linke's clear stance on Palestine and anti-fascism, despite potential electoral costs, demonstrates this approach.

2. Integrating diverse struggles within class analysis Feminist, climate, anti-racist, and LGBTQIA+ struggles must be centred within the broader class struggle, rejecting the false division between class and identity issues. This counters both the intellectual retreat that abandons oppressed groups and the sectarian tendency to hierarchy struggles.

3. Building power from below through concrete engagement This requires continuous presence and visible work in communities and workplaces. Die Linke's "heating costs campaign" exemplifies how revolutionary organisations can build trust through immediate material improvements while advancing broader political goals.

4. Key tactical lesson: The success of "lighthouse models" like Leipzig and Neukölln demonstrate how mass participatory work can be achieved from below, creating replicable organising methods.

5. Developing transitional programs that connect immediate and long-term goals Effective programs must mobilise people around tangible improvements while building towards systemic transformation. This goes beyond mere "problem-solving" to provide a compelling vision of post-capitalist society.

6. Building revolutionary organisation as theory-practice mediation Such organisations preserve the memory of struggles, draw collective lessons, and prepare for future battles. This involves training cadres, engaging in political education, and unifying fragmented forces—exactly what Die Linke achieved through its "participatory offensive."

7. Advancing ecosocialist alternatives This prioritises human needs over profit, advocates for democratic planning and self-management, and systematically challenges capitalism's growth imperative. It requires "industrial reconstruction" of key sectors towards socially useful production.

International Applications: From Germany to Global Strategy

These strategic insights apply beyond Germany's specific context. Similar patterns of intellectual retreat appear in:

- France: Where parts of the left accommodate nationalist rhetoric around immigration
- Britain: Where some leftists have retreated into "left-conservative" positions on social issues
- United States: Where segments of the left have adopted class-reductionist positions that abandon anti-racism

Meanwhile, sectarian fragmentation appears in:

- France's NPA split between "open" and "closed" revolutionary models
- Britain's persistent revolutionary left divisions that prioritise ideological purity over mass engagement
- Spain's Podemos fragmentation over strategic and tactical differences
- The principled alternative-building model offers concrete lessons for movements facing similar choices:
- For established left parties: Die Linke's experience shows that principled positions, combined with grassroots engagement, can rebuild membership and influence even after major splits.
- For revolutionary organisations: The importance of patient, consistent work in communities and workplaces, rather than seeking shortcuts through electoral tactics or ideological correctness.
- For movement activists: The necessity of connecting immediate struggles to longer-term strategic goals while maintaining clear anti-capitalist analysis.

Conclusion: Building Socialist Alternatives in the Age of Crisis

The urgency of principled alternative-building is amplified by our planetary polycrisis, where interconnected economic, social, ecological, and existential crises threaten to strengthen authoritarian leaders worldwide. The AfD's success in Germany is just one manifestation of a global pattern where fascist movements capitalise on left weakness and fragmentation.

Overcoming this requires what Die Linke demonstrates: that unwavering principles, combined with concrete engagement, can build effective resistance even under adverse conditions. The party's 60,000 new members didn't join because of tactical flexibility or ideological purity, but because they saw an organisation that stood for clear principles while doing practical work in their communities.

The task before international socialists is to unite fragmented forces globally, challenging both the illusions of "intellectual retreat" and the impotence of "sectarian bunkers." We must tirelessly work where the masses are, building "red-green" coalitions that can advance ecosocialist alternatives to capitalism's destructive trajectory.

As conditions become increasingly dire, "the conditions for ecosocialist transitions may be slowly ripening." This makes the consistent, organised pursuit of anti-capitalist, internationalist, and democratic alternatives not just desirable, but an absolute necessity for humanity's future. Die Linke's "lighthouse model" shows this is possible—now we must build similar beacons of resistance across the globe.

The choice facing today's left is stark: retreat into accommodation with the far-right, isolate ourselves in sectarian purity, or build principled alternatives that can actually win. The German experience shows us which path leads to victory.

Ireland: In Defence of People Before Profit's Comprehensive Marxist Approach to Oppression

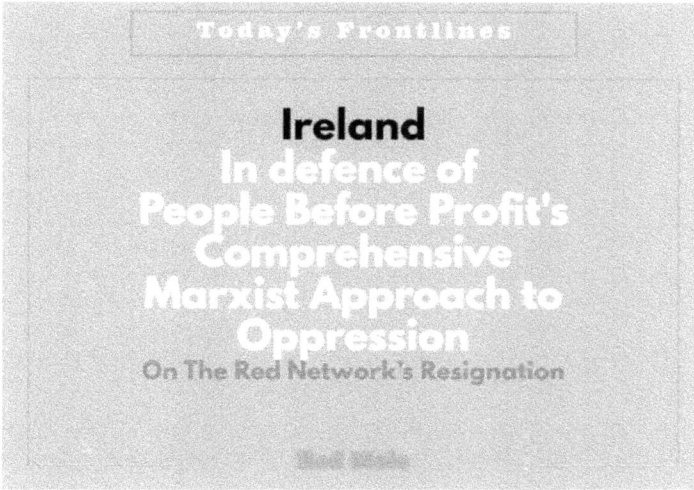

The struggle against all forms of oppression is not a distraction from class war, but an essential part of it.

The Red Network's statement, "Why The Red Network Has Left People Before Profit," contrasts "class war" with "culture war," arguing that focusing on social issues ("student moralism," "performative politics," "moralising") is divisive and ineffective. That strategic conception is key to its political difference with PBP. The Red Network's statement makes other points about PBP, some concerning. If those were resolved, its political differences would still justify the network's separation. This position reflects a narrow focus that is challenged by a comprehensive Marxist approach, which argues that the fight against various forms of oppression is not separate from or secondary to the class struggle, but is in fact an integral and necessary component of it [Thanks to a post about the departure by The Cedar Lounge Revolution, we can recommend you read the Irish Independent's interview with Dublin councillor Madeleine Johansson, who is part of the Network].

Capitalism does not merely involve class exploitation; it actively utilises and reinforces various forms of oppression. Oppressions based on race, gender, sexuality, and caste are not accidental but are deeply embedded within capitalist social relations and are actively reproduced by the system. As Arya Meroni notes, capitalist society possesses an entire economic, ideological, political, and cultural apparatus to maintain its power, and building a new class consciousness necessitates integrating and respecting all sectors and struggles of the working class

.

Capitalism Thrives on All Oppressions

The ruling class benefits significantly from these divisions, employing them to suppress wages, weaken collective power, and pit segments of the working class against each other. Historically and currently, the ruling class uses strategies to divide the working class along lines such as race, gender, ethnicity, language, and religion. To ignore or downplay the fight against these oppressions, as the Red Network's "class war not culture war" framing tends to do, is to misunderstand how capitalism functions and inadvertently aids the oppressors by leaving the working class divided.

Furthermore, oppression can occur within the working class itself. This manifests as racism, sexism, LGBTQI+phobia, and other prejudices. A powerful, united working-class movement cannot be built by ignoring or attempting to bypass these internal divisions. Instead, it must actively confront and combat these prejudices, standing as the "tribune of the people" that fights against all forms of tyranny and outrage, not just economic ones. As Lenin argued in relation to economism, any and every manifestation of police tyranny and autocratic outrage is a means to draw the masses into the political struggle. True solidarity is built by fighting all oppressions as part of the common struggle against the system that produces them.

Autonomous Struggles Strengthen the Movement

The self-organisation of oppressed groups – such as feminist, anti-racist, and LGBTQI+ movements – is not a deviation from unity or mere "moralism," but a vital step towards building a broader, more effective movement. These autonomous movements often arise in response to the limitations and biases within broader movements, including those on the left, which may fail to address specific experiences of oppression adequately. They are crucial for developing analyses specific to particular oppressions, building solidarity among those directly affected, and challenging ingrained prejudices within the working class itself. Dismissing these struggles as "student moralism" risks alienating working-class people who experience these oppressions daily and prevents the building of the comprehensive movement needed to challenge the interlocking systems of oppression and their material roots within capitalist social relations. At its best, the slogan "the personal is political" highlighted the need to understand individual experiences of oppression as rooted in broader social, economic, cultural, and political structures, aiming to politicise personal problems and foster collective action, not merely individual lifestyle choices.

Integrating Liberation into the Class Struggle

A comprehensive Marxist approach integrates the fight against specific oppressions into a comprehensive struggle against the capitalist system. Concepts like "Feminism for the 99%" exemplify this synthesis, aiming for a class-based feminist movement that understands the interconnectedness of gender, race, and economic exploitation. This framework explicitly rejects the idea that fighting oppression is separate from the fight for socialism. It seeks to forge a truly revolutionary force capable of achieving the liberation of all by focusing on the shared struggle against the interlocking systems of oppression and their material roots within capitalist social relations.

The Red Network's critique suggests that class struggle will automatically pull in those who disagree on social issues, an approach sadly disproven by the experience of the last several decades. While common struggle can build solidarity and challenge prejudices, relying solely on this without actively combating oppressive ideas within the class is insufficient and ignores the depth of these divisions that capitalism actively reinforces (not the least, including the division of the north of Ireland). The task is to actively link anti-oppression struggles to the class struggle, not to wait for the latter to somehow resolve the former.

Rethinking Strategy and PBP's Approach

In passing, the Red Network's statement makes two notable choices in its critique of People Before Profit (PBP).

Firstly, it seems to frame PBP as if it is attempting and failing to be a specific type of revolutionary vanguard party (perhaps Leninist), highlighting perceived failures in leadership development, political education, and adherence to a strict programmatic line. In practice, PBP operates more as a broad anticapitalist party, aiming to unite diverse political trends. Critiquing it based on criteria it may not set for itself is arguably an uncharitable interpretation.

Secondly, the statement claims that PBP doesn't have a "party programme" and that its demands are merely expressions of current struggles. Yet, the PBP manifesto outlines a vision for a "32-county eco-socialist republic" and details a range of specific policies across various areas like housing, healthcare, environment, and anti-racism. While not necessarily presented in the traditional "minimum/maximum" format critiqued by the Red Network, this document clearly contains elements of a programme, outlining both immediate demands and a broader societal goal. This suggests a difference in interpretation of what constitutes a "programme" and the strategic function of a party like PBP compared to the Red Network's specific criteria.

Ultimately, a comprehensive Marxist approach argues that the fight against oppression is not a sideline but an essential front in the class war. A genuinely revolutionary force capable of achieving the liberation of all must integrate the struggles against specific oppressions into a comprehensive struggle against the capitalist system that thrives on division. Dismissing the fight against oppression as mere "culture war" plays into the hands of the very system the Red Network seeks to overthrow.

International Left Strategy

'We Want Russia to Lose' vs. 'All Nationalism is Poison'

A bitter divide over Ukraine has profoundly fractured the European Left, with Russian socialists demanding their own government's defeat while other revolutionary groups condemn specific factions as "enemies of our class". This is not an abstract theoretical debate but a live, unfolding organizational crisis: precisely the kind of contemporary struggle that defines the strategic challenges for socialist movements today. In an accompanying podcast (linked here: listen online) we outline the debate: in the article below, we delve deeper.

The recent positions articulated by Dmitrii Kovalev, in an interview published on 12 April 2025, following a "Solidarity with Ukraine" Conference in Brussels in late March, starkly contrast with the universal defeatism espoused by groups like Community of Fight and a dangerous misrepresentation of the Leninist position advanced by the Revolutionary Communist Party of Canada. This ideological chasm is actively fracturing socialist organizations across the continent, from Die Linke in Germany to broader international networks, positioning itself as a defining strategic crisis for the contemporary left.

This immediate, ongoing conflict demands a re-evaluation of core principles in the face of imperialist aggression and national liberation struggles, highlighting the urgent need for clarity within revolutionary organizations.

The Immediate Crisis: Three Paths to Revolutionary Defeatism, Three Fatal Missteps?

At the heart of this organizational conflict lie three fundamentally opposed interpretations of revolutionary defeatism concerning the war in Ukraine. This division reflects deeper strategic questions about how revolutionary organizations should apply historical Marxist principles to contemporary conflicts.

The Russian Revolutionary Position: Selective Defeatism

Dmitrii Kovalev, representing the Left for Peace without Annexations, Russia, advocates for revolutionary defeatism specifically against his own government. His coalition, which includes various socialist, Trotskyist, and Maoist organizations, unequivocally declares: "we want Russia to lose this war". Their vision requires "going back to Ukraine's original borders, without any annexations," and they call for "the destruction of the present Russian Federation". This is concrete political practice: activists inside Russia "agitate for defeatism" while finding support from a faction within the German party Die Linke. The Russian Socialist Movement (RSM) echoes this, calling for the "military defeat of Putin's regime," viewing it as "reactionary authoritarian capitalism" and an "enemy of all forms of democracy".

Universal Defeatism: All Sides Are Imperialist

Groups like Community of Fight (aligned to the League of Internationalist Communists) reject any distinction between the warring parties. Their manifesto presents Revolutionary Defeatism as 'The Only Alternative to Imperialist War', and argues that the conflict involves a "greater number of states" in a "massacre of Ukrainian and Russian proletarians for the defense of their geopolitical interests". From this perspective, "all nationalism is poison," and "all defense of the national bourgeoisie implies the negation of class independence". They explicitly name Ukrainian anarchist militias like "RevDia, Black Flag or Black Headquarter" and support networks like "Solidarity Collectives" as "enemies of our class" for keeping Russian and Ukrainian proletarians killing each other for "bourgeois interests".

Fake Leninist Defeatism: Inter-Imperialist Conflict

The Revolutionary Communist Party of Canada, part of the Revolutionary Communist International led by Alan Woods, presents what it claims as authentic Leninist defeatism. In a facebook video, they argue: "there are a lot of differences between the war in Ukraine and World War One, but they are both conflicts between rival imperialists. This war is both Russia versus NATO." They advocate the classical position: "turn your guns on the ruling class" and insist "our main enemy is at home." For Western socialists, this means fighting their own ruling class rather than supporting either side. Their analysis treats Ukraine's defense as equivalent to inter-imperialist warfare, concluding that

Ukrainian workers should "fight their corrupt capitalist oligarchy" rather than the Russian invaders.

This represents a significant revision of Lenin's actual support for national liberation struggles of oppressed nations against imperialism. The RCP-Canada position equates Ukraine's just defense against Russia's imperialist colonial war with an inter-imperialist conflict. Can you imagine Lenin advising Irish revolution in 1916 not to fight the British, but to turn their guns on the frail Irish capitalist class rather than pursue the struggle for independence?

Organizational Fractures Across the International Left

These competing interpretations create significant fractures within European and international socialist organizations:

Die Linke in Germany faces internal struggles, with a faction supporting Kovalev's line while the party congress adopted a complex resolution demanding Russian troop withdrawal and sanctions, yet notably failing to take a clear stand on Ukrainian self-defense. This reflects deep-seated pacifist traditions challenged by Russian aggression.

The Revolutionary Communist International, as seen in its Canadian section, promotes the "fake Leninist" position that treats Ukraine as part of an inter-imperialist conflict. This ultra-left tendency's analysis fundamentally misapplies Lenin's WWI defeatism to a national liberation struggle, creating confusion within Trotskyist networks internationally.

Other German Trotskyist currents, such as Arbeitermacht, align with the "No War but Class War: Neither Russia nor NATO!" position, viewing the conflict "solely as a proxy war between the two imperialist powers."

The Fourth International actively champions "unconditional solidarity with Ukrainian resistance to Russian imperialism," viewing the war as an "imperialist attempt by the neo-fascist Putin regime to annexe Ukraine, while the people of Ukraine are fighting for national liberation, independence, and democracy."

Strategic Stakes: Theoretical Confusion and Organizational Crisis

This three-way split reveals more than tactical disagreements: it exposes fundamental confusion about applying Marxist anti-imperialist theory to contemporary conflicts. The choices made directly impact revolutionary organizations' capacity for effective solidarity work and strategic clarity.

The Revolutionary Communist International's position particularly demonstrates dangerous theoretical drift. By treating Ukraine's national liberation struggle as inter-imperialist warfare, they abandon Lenin's actual method of distinguishing between oppressor and oppressed nations. This "ultra-left" deviation leads to practical abstention from solidarity with the oppressed, masked as revolutionary purity.

The organizational consequences are severe. Groups claiming the same Leninist heritage reach contradictory strategic conclusions about basic solidarity work. Should revolutionaries support arms for Ukraine's defense? Should they organize material aid for Ukrainian resistance? The theoretical confusion translates into organizational paralysis and strategic incoherence.

Analytical Framework: Lenin's Defeatism and Contemporary Misapplications

Hal Draper's "The Myth of Lenin's 'Revolutionary Defeatism'" provides crucial analytical tools for understanding both the historical complexities of the concept and why its contemporary applications often miss the mark.

Lenin's original "defeatism" against Tsarism during the Russo-Japanese War (1904-05) and World War I was based on viewing the defeat of Russia's particularly reactionary government as the "lesser evil" that could facilitate revolutionary change. However, this position "met with the widest opposition in the ranks of the Bolshevik party itself" due to its apparent contradiction: if Russian socialists wished for Russia's defeat, what distinguished them from German socialists wishing the same outcome?

Crucially, Lenin abandoned the defeat-slogan entirely in 1917 after the March Revolution overthrew Tsarism. He found it "incompatible with a living Marxist approach to the problem of the defense of the nation" and realized his previous approach had been "too abstract." The democratic revolution "erased the rock-bottom motive" for the "special Russian consideration" of Tsarism as the "unique menace."

More importantly for contemporary debates, Lenin himself made crucial distinctions that the Revolutionary Communist International ignores. Even during his most "defeatist" period, Lenin argued that Marxists would "wish the oppressed, dependent and unequal states victory over the oppressor, slaveholding and predatory 'Great' Powers." This principle directly contradicts treating Ukraine's anti-colonial struggle as inter-imperialist warfare.

The historical record shows Lenin supporting national liberation movements against imperial oppression, from Ireland against Britain to colonial peoples against their imperial masters. The RCP-Canada's position represents a mechanical application of WWI formulations that Lenin himself abandoned and that contradicts his broader method of analyzing oppressor-oppressed relationships.

Lessons for Today: Navigating National Liberation vs. Inter-Imperialist Conflict

The three-way organizational split over Ukraine reveals the urgent need for theoretical clarity about distinguishing between different types of conflicts:

Ukraine as National Liberation Struggle: Ukraine is not an imperialist power but an oppressed nation fighting for self-determination against Russian imperialism. Ukrainian socialists in Sotsialnyi Rukh explicitly resist the "imperialist attempt by the neo-fascist Putin regime to annex Ukraine." The reality of murder, rape, and torture under Russian occupation demonstrates the colonial character of Putin's war.

The Oppressor-Oppressed Distinction: Revolutionary internationalism demands unconditional solidarity with oppressed nations fighting for liberation. To argue for defeatism against Ukraine's struggle constitutes "passive complicity with the imperialist aggressor" and "objectively helps the stronger, oppressive side." This aligns with Lenin's actual method of supporting dependent states against predatory powers.

Rejecting Ultra-Left Abstention: The Revolutionary Communist International's position exemplifies dangerous ultra-left deviation that abandons concrete solidarity under the guise of revolutionary purity. Their mechanical application of WWI defeatism to Ukraine's anti-colonial struggle represents precisely the kind of abstract theorizing Lenin rejected after 1917.

The "Main Enemy at Home" Principle Applied Correctly: For Russian socialists, the main enemy is unequivocally Putin's regime, requiring active work for its defeat. For Western socialists, the main enemy includes their own governments' imperialism, but not by denying Ukraine's right to self-defense or necessary aid. The principle means opposing your own imperialism while supporting victims of other imperialisms.

Building Revolutionary Organizations: The task requires developing clear theoretical frameworks that distinguish between supporting national liberation struggles and opposing inter-imperialist wars. Revolutionary organizations need strategic clarity about when to apply defeatism (against your own imperialist state) and when to provide solidarity (with oppressed nations fighting for liberation).

The current organizational crisis over "revolutionary defeatism" in the European Left highlights the dangers of mechanical theoretical application divorced from concrete analysis. The Revolutionary Communist International's treatment of Ukraine's anti-colonial struggle as inter-imperialist conflict represents a significant theoretical regression that abandons Lenin's actual method. Russian socialists must advocate for their own state's defeat while international revolutionaries must unequivocally support Ukraine's national liberation struggle. Only through this dual approach can revolutionary organizations maintain both principled anti-imperialism and effective solidarity with the oppressed.

Beyond Bambery's "Peace At Any Cost": Why US-Russia Talks On Ukraine Are A Dangerous Fantasy

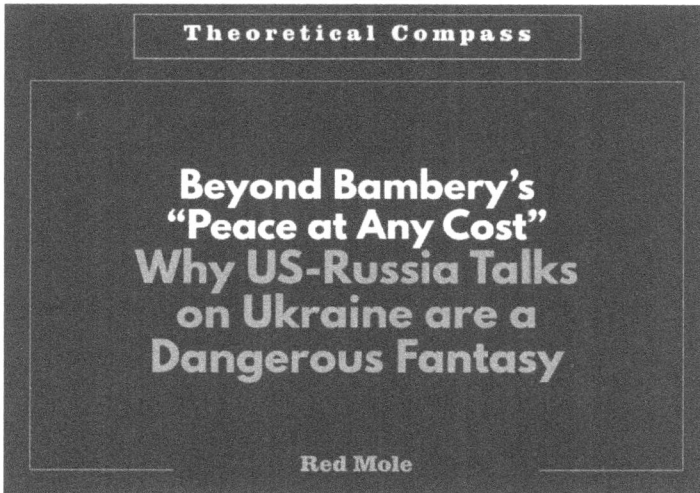

Chris Bambery's assertion that "US-Russia peace talks would be a good plan" and his dismissal of those who believe in a "pipedream of a Ukrainian victory" represent a perspective that many on the Left profoundly challenge. Far from being a path to peace, such negotiations, especially without Ukraine's full, uncompromised participation, are viewed as a "robber's peace" designed to serve imperial interests and set the stage for future conflicts.

Here's why Bambery's position is deeply problematic:
THE EXCLUSION AND BETRAYAL OF UKRAINE

Bambery's argument hinges on the idea that Putin "is winning" and can dictate terms. However, proposals for US-Russia peace talks are heavily criticised for excluding and humiliating the Ukrainian government and people. Sources indicate that such talks often involve Trump and Putin "carving Ukraine up" for their own imperialist interests, with demands for significant portions of Ukrainian territory and resources without offering genuine security guarantees. The principle of "Nothing about Ukraine without Ukraine" is paramount, asserting that only the Ukrainian people, who are enduring the conflict, have the right to decide their path forward. Any "peace" imposed against their will would merely be a "prelude to more occupation and violence in the future".

Furthermore, there are accusations that Western powers, including the US and UK, have previously "sabotaged" peace talks that might have been more favourable to Ukraine, precisely because they aimed to prolong the war to weaken Russia. This demonstrates that external powers manipulate the conflict for their own geopolitical advantage, rather than genuinely seeking a just resolution for Ukraine.

THE WAR AS A JUST STRUGGLE FOR NATIONAL SELF-DEFENCE

Bambery's framing of the conflict as merely a "meatgrinder of a war" or implying it's a "proxy war" for Western interests denies the fundamental character of the conflict as a just struggle for national self-determination against an imperialist aggressor. The narrative that Ukraine is simply a proxy for US imperialism is explicitly rejected as "Kremlin-influenced mythology" and a "hoax".

Instead, the sources emphasize that Russia's invasion is an "imperialist attempt by the neo-fascist Putin regime to annex Ukraine," challenging international law and legitimate national existence. Ukrainian popular resistance and resilience are highlighted as key factors that have thwarted Russia's initial plans. To deny Ukraine's right to resist and receive necessary weapons, as some "pacifist" positions do, effectively leads to "acquiescence in the face of the Russian attack and an appeasement of it".

THE PITFALLS OF "FALSE PACIFISM" AND "CAMPISM"

Bambery's call for "peace talks" without conditions aligns with what is termed "false pacifism". This approach must be criticized for:

- Being egocentric, prioritising opposition to one's national government over genuine solidarity with the Ukrainian people.
- Refusing to "recognise the imperialist character of the war waged by the Kremlin" and attempting to portray it merely as a response to NATO expansion.
- Ignoring the demands of Ukrainian and Russian socialists who insist on rejecting any compromises with Putin's regime and approving arms transfers to Ukraine.

Bambery's perspective also falls into campism, which simplifies global conflicts into a binary opposition between "western imperialism" (led by the US) and an "anti-imperialist" camp (including Russia and China), often leading to ignoring or defending the authoritarian and imperialist actions of non-Western states. This "pseudo-anti-imperialism" means turning a blind eye to Russian imperialism, its nationalist rhetoric, and its crimes.

The concept of "the enemy is at home," while historically relevant in inter-imperialist wars, crudely copied and pasted onto a much more complex situation like Ukraine's war of national self-defence.

RUSSIA'S IMPERIALIST AMBITIONS AND BRUTAL REALITY

1. Bambery claims Putin "is winning" and implies Russia should be "brought in from the cold". However, Russian imperial ambitions are explicitly condemned:
2. Putin's regime is neo-fascist, employing nationalist, xenophobic, and even genocidal rhetoric and practices.
3. Russia's "denazification" claim is identified as a propaganda tool to

justify the war and "annihilate Ukraine".

4. Putin's vision of a "multipolarity" is not a progressive alternative but one where only a "limited number of large states will have any voice in the international arena," essentially a recipe for "competing capitalist authoritarianisms".

5. The war is consistently presented as an effort to "tighten control over Russian society and crush all dissent," leading to severe repression of anti-war activists, socialists, and feminists.

6. Russian claims of Ukrainian protests being anti-war are "false and misrepresent the actual use of Western funds", designed to "undermine Ukraine's legitimacy and discourage Western support".

A Principled Anti-Imperialist Stance

While vehemently condemning Bambery's "campist" position, a principled Left stance also critically assesses the actions of Western powers. This means:

- Denouncing Western imperialism's strategic goals and the "militaristic conception of security".
- Critiquing the hypocrisy of Western politicians who condemn Russian aggression but facilitate Israeli actions in Gaza.
- Calling for unconditional solidarity with Ukrainian resistance and their right to receive weapons for self-defence from any source, without endorsing the policies of their government or NATO.
- Opposing the neoliberal agenda imposed on Ukraine by Western and EU institutions.

Chris Bambery offers a dangerous simplification that ignores the agency of the Ukrainian people, the imperialist nature of Russia's aggression, and the complexities of global power dynamics. For socialists committed to liberation, the path to peace lies not in enabling a "robber's peace" between imperial powers, but in unconditional solidarity with the oppressed, a consistent fight against all forms of imperialism, and the demand for a just peace rooted in self-determination and social justice for the Ukrainian people.

'Imperialist Economism' and Ukraine: Why Self-Determination Matters For Socialist Strategy

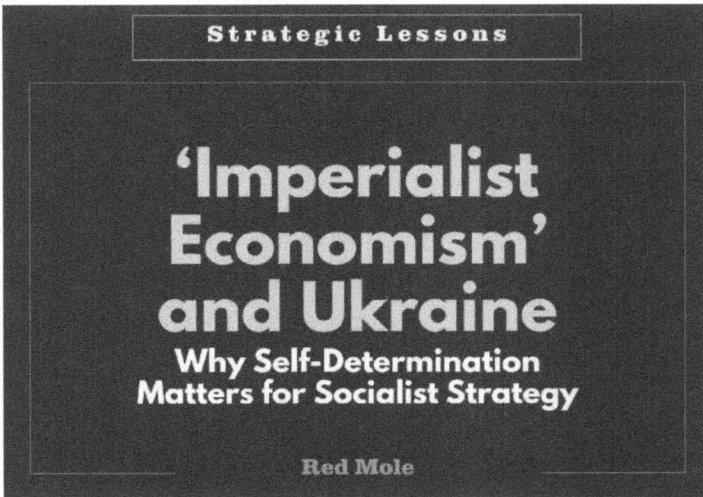

Strategic Lessons

'Imperialist Economism' and Ukraine

Why Self-Determination Matters for Socialist Strategy

Red Mole

Strategic Lesson for Revolutionary Organizing: Lenin's critique of "imperialist economism" provides essential tools for analyzing contemporary national liberation struggles, showing why revolutionary movements must support concrete democratic struggles rather than waiting for abstract economic transformation.

Introduction: The Theoretical Stakes

The recent exposure of analytical bankruptcy in segments of the far left around Ukraine has deeper theoretical roots than opportunistic position-taking or camp-following. It reflects a fundamental misunderstanding of the relationship between democratic struggles and socialist revolution, an error Lenin identified and comprehensively critiqued during World War I as "imperialist economism." Understanding this critique is essential for building revolutionary organizations capable of principled international solidarity in an era of shifting imperial alignments.

Lenin's analysis offers contemporary revolutionaries crucial insights for navigating the complex terrain of national liberation movements in a multipolar world. His framework demonstrates why supporting democratic struggles against immediate oppression strengthens rather than weakens the broader anti-capitalist movement, providing theoretical grounding for positions that might otherwise appear contradictory or opportunistic.

Lenin's Historical Context: The WWI Debates

During the catastrophic years of 1914-1916, European socialism faced its greatest crisis since the Paris Commune. The collapse of the Second International into competing national chauvinisms forced revolutionary Marxists to fundamentally reconsider their theoretical frameworks. Within this broader crisis, a specific debate emerged around the national question that would prove crucial for understanding imperialism's political dynamics.

The context was urgent and concrete. The war had revealed the inadequacy of pre-war socialist positions on both imperialism and national liberation. Russian revolutionaries like Nikolai Bukharin and P. Kievsky (Yury Pyatakov) developed what they considered a more "advanced" analysis: since imperialism represented capitalism's highest stage, traditional democratic demands including national self-determination had become historically obsolete. Only direct socialist revolution could resolve the contradictions capitalism had created.

This position appeared sophisticated and "scientifically" rigorous. Its proponents argued that supporting national liberation movements under imperialism was at best naive and at worst reactionary, since such movements inevitably served the interests of competing imperialist powers. Better to focus exclusively on the "real" task: organizing the working class for socialist revolution in the advanced capitalist countries.

Lenin's response was both immediate and comprehensive. In a series of articles written throughout 1916, including "The Nascent Trend of Imperialist Economism," "Reply to P. Kievsky," and "A Caricature of Marxism and Imperialist Economism," he systematically demolished what he saw as a fundamental theoretical error with dangerous political consequences.

The Core Error: Democracy versus Economic Determinism

Lenin's critique focused on the relationship between democratic and socialist struggles. The imperialist economists, he argued, had made the same fundamental error as their predecessors in the 1894-1902 "economistic" tendency: reducing all political questions to narrow economic calculations while ignoring the concrete tasks of building revolutionary consciousness and organization.

The specific error was methodological. As Lenin wrote in his reply to Kievsky: "Capitalism has triumphed—therefore there is no need to bother with political problems, the old Economists reasoned in 1894-1901, falling into rejection of the political struggle in Russia. Imperialism has triumphed— therefore there is no need to bother with the problems of political democracy, reason the present-day imperialist Economists."

This represented what Lenin called "just as complete a misinterpretation of the relationship between socialism and democracy" as the earlier economism. The imperialist economists failed to understand that democratic struggles served essential functions for revolutionary organizing, regardless of whether they could be "fully" achieved under capitalism.

Lenin's key insight: "All 'democracy' consists in the proclamation and realisation of 'rights' which under capitalism are realisable only to a very small degree and only relatively. But without the proclamation of these rights, without a struggle to introduce them now, immediately, without training the masses in the spirit of this struggle, socialism is impossible."

The National Question as Democratic Struggle

Applied to the national question, this analysis had profound implications. Lenin argued that the right to national self-determination was not primarily about creating more nation-states, but about building the international solidarity necessary for successful socialist revolution.

The logic was dialectical rather than mechanical. National oppression created divisions within the international working class that served ruling-class interests in both oppressor and oppressed nations. Workers in oppressor nations who believed they benefited from their own government's colonial expansion would be less likely to make common cause with workers from oppressed nations. Meanwhile, workers in oppressed nations who faced national persecution alongside economic exploitation would justifiably distrust socialist movements that ignored or minimized their specific oppression.

Supporting the right to self-determination served to overcome these divisions by proving to oppressed nations that socialists in oppressor countries genuinely opposed all forms of imperialism, not just economic exploitation. This built the trust necessary for voluntary international unity after revolutionary victory.

Crucially, this right was tactical rather than absolute. Lenin emphasized: "The national question is always subordinate to the class question." The goal was not endless balkanization but unified international socialism. However, such unity could only be achieved through voluntary association based on genuine equality, not imposed through continued domination by formerly oppressive powers.

Concrete Analysis: The Irish Easter Rising

Lenin's defense of the 1916 Irish Easter Rising provides the clearest example of his methodology in practice. The rebellion was widely criticized by some European socialists as a "putsch" and "petty-bourgeois movement" that lacked sufficient proletarian character to merit support. More damaging, the Irish nationalists had accepted aid from Germany, Britain's imperial rival, leading some socialists to dismiss the uprising as mere German manipulation.

Lenin's response cut through these abstract objections to focus on concrete political effects. The uprising "delivered a blow against the power of the English imperialist bourgeoisie" regardless of its class composition or the source of its external aid. To expect a "pure" social revolution was "a fundamental mistake," since real liberation movements necessarily involve "the petty bourgeoisie with all its prejudices."

The key criterion was maintaining political independence while accepting tactical aid. Lenin acknowledged that imperialist powers would "utilize any national and revolutionary movement in the enemy camp" but argued this tactical reality didn't negate the political significance of genuine liberation struggles. The legitimacy was determined by objective effect, not donor motives or ideological purity.

This analysis extended to other historical precedents: the American Revolution accepting French aid, various colonial movements receiving support from rival imperial powers, and liberation movements navigating between competing great power interests. In each case, the decisive factor was whether the movement maintained its own political goals and class independence.

The Serbian Counterexample: When National Struggles Serve Imperialism

Lenin's analysis was nuanced rather than formulaic. Not all movements claiming national liberation deserved support. His critique of Serbian participation in World War I demonstrated how ostensibly national struggles could be subordinated to broader imperialist projects.

From a formal perspective, Austria-Hungary's attack on Serbia appeared to justify Serbian "national defense." Serbia had legitimate grievances and a long history of liberation struggle against Ottoman and Austrian domination. However, Lenin concluded this was not a genuine national liberation struggle worthy of socialist support.

The reason was structural rather than moral. The war was not "isolated" but served as "prologue to a universal, European war" with "clearly pronounced imperialist character." The "national" phraseology was a "fable" designed to mobilize popular support for what was fundamentally an inter-imperialist conflict for territorial division and plunder.

This analysis provided crucial criteria for distinguishing genuine liberation struggles from imperialist manipulations:

- Was the struggle primarily about overthrowing immediate oppression or serving broader great power competition?
- Did the movement maintain genuine political independence or function as a proxy?
- Could success reasonably be expected to advance democratic rights and working-class interests?

Contemporary Applications: Ukraine Through Lenin's Framework

Applying Lenin's analytical framework to contemporary Ukraine reveals why principled support for Ukrainian resistance is theoretically consistent with anti-imperialism rather than contradictory to it. The analysis requires examining concrete political dynamics rather than abstract theoretical categories.

Ukraine faces what Lenin would recognize as a classic colonial invasion: Russia's explicit goal is re-establishing imperial control over territory it considers historically subordinate. Russian ideological justifications explicitly deny Ukrainian national legitimacy, describing it as an artificial "creation of Lenin" populated by people fit only for "prostitution and cleaning toilets" in Europe. This represents the "Great Russian chauvinism" Lenin consistently opposed.

The Trump test validates Ukrainian independence rather than undermining it. If Ukraine were merely a US proxy, as "inter-imperialist" analysis claims, Ukrainian resistance should have collapsed when Trump demanded territorial concessions and threatened aid cuts. Instead, Ukrainian determination persisted regardless of shifting American positions, demonstrating genuine national agency.

External aid follows the Irish Easter Rising pattern rather than the Serbian model. While Ukraine accepts military assistance from NATO powers, it maintains political independence and pursues goals (territorial integrity, democratic development, European integration) that serve Ukrainian rather than American interests. The aid enables resistance against immediate oppression rather than advancing broader imperialist conquest.

The class dynamics also align with Lenin's framework. Ukrainian resistance includes significant working-class participation and has strengthened rather than weakened democratic organization within Ukraine. The movement's primary demand is ending foreign occupation, a democratic task that advances rather than hinders international working-class solidarity.

Organizational Implications for Today's Left

Lenin's critique of imperialist economism offers crucial lessons for contemporary revolutionary organizing. The fundamental insight remains valid: movements that cannot support concrete democratic struggles against immediate oppression will be unable to build the international solidarity necessary for broader transformation.

Revolutionary organizations need analytical frameworks sophisticated enough to distinguish between genuine liberation movements and imperialist proxies without falling into rigid formulas that ignore changing conditions. This requires developing what Lenin called "concrete analysis of concrete conditions" rather than abstract theoretical categories applied mechanically across different situations.

The methodological approach is dialectical: support democratic struggles while maintaining political independence from all imperial powers. This means supporting Ukrainian resistance while opposing NATO expansion, backing Palestinian liberation while critiquing authoritarian allies, defending Cuban sovereignty while supporting internal democratization efforts.

Contemporary imperialist economism manifests in different forms than Lenin's opponents but displays identical underlying logic: reducing political questions to economic determinism, evading concrete solidarity tasks through abstract theoretical formulations, and ultimately serving ruling-class interests through pseudo-radical inaction.

Organizations falling into this trap find themselves unable to respond coherently to shifting conditions, as the Trump test dramatically demonstrated. Static frameworks collapse when imperial powers reverse positions, leaving movements either trapped in obsolete analysis or constantly adjusting positions based on ruling-class politics rather than principled commitments.

Building Independent International Analysis

The alternative Lenin advocated remains essential: developing independent working-class positions based on consistent anti-imperialist principles rather than reflexive opposition to currently dominant powers. This requires five organizational commitments:

1. Principled Solidarity: Support liberation struggles against immediate oppressors regardless of which powers currently provide aid or which theoretical tendencies advocate similar positions. The criterion is objective effect on democratic rights and working-class organization, not donor identity or analytical pedigree.

2. Concrete Analysis: Examine specific conditions of each struggle rather than applying abstract formulas. Distinguish between genuine liberation movements maintaining political independence and proxy forces serving imperial interests, recognizing this distinction can change as conditions evolve.

3. Democratic Struggle: Understand that supporting democratic demands strengthens rather than weakens socialist organizing by building the international trust and working-class confidence necessary for revolutionary transformation.

4. Theoretical Flexibility: Develop analytical frameworks robust enough to handle shifting conditions without abandoning fundamental principles. Avoid both rigid formulism and opportunistic position-adjustment based on immediate tactical calculations.

5. Historical Consciousness: Learn from past theoretical debates to avoid repeating errors that have already been identified and resolved. Lenin's critique of imperialist economism provides tested tools for navigating contemporary challenges.

The Broader Strategic Framework

Lenin's analysis of the national question was part of a comprehensive strategy for revolutionary transformation in the imperialist epoch. He understood that successful socialism required genuinely international organization, which could only be achieved through voluntary unity based on demonstrated solidarity with oppressed peoples.

This strategic insight remains crucial for contemporary organizing. In an era of intensifying inter-imperial competition, revolutionary movements face constant pressure to choose sides between competing power blocs. The imperialist economist response is to focus exclusively on opposing one's "own" imperialism while treating other liberation struggles as distractions or manipulations.

Lenin's alternative approach recognizes that building international working-class solidarity requires active support for all genuine liberation struggles, regardless of complex geopolitical contexts. This doesn't mean uncritical support for any movement claiming progressive credentials, but rather developing sophisticated analysis capable of distinguishing liberation from manipulation while maintaining principled solidarity with the oppressed.

The Ukraine case demonstrates how this approach works in practice. Supporting Ukrainian resistance against Russian colonialism strengthens international anti-imperialist solidarity by proving that principled anti-imperialism opposes all forms of imperial domination, not just Western varieties. This builds trust with oppressed peoples globally while exposing the bankruptcy of both liberal hawks who support imperialism when convenient and pseudo-anti-imperialists who oppose it only selectively.

Conclusion: Democracy as Revolutionary Strategy

Lenin's critique of imperialist economism provides essential theoretical tools for contemporary revolutionary organizing. His central insight—that democratic struggles strengthen rather than weaken socialist transformation— offers crucial guidance for navigating the complex terrain of national liberation in a multipolar world.

The theoretical stakes couldn't be higher. Organizations that cannot develop principled positions on concrete liberation struggles will find themselves marginalized from the real movements reshaping global politics. The alternative to imperialist economism is not opportunistic position-taking but theoretically grounded solidarity based on consistent anti-imperialist principles.

Understanding why self-determination matters for socialist strategy requires grasping the dialectical relationship between democratic and economic struggles. Revolutionary transformation needs both the international solidarity that comes from supporting oppressed peoples and the organizational experience that comes from democratic struggle against immediate oppression.

Lenin's framework provides tested methods for building such organizations: concrete analysis of specific conditions, principled solidarity with liberation movements maintaining political independence, and theoretical flexibility capable of adapting to changing circumstances without abandoning fundamental commitments.

The contemporary left faces the same choice Lenin's generation confronted: develop analytical frameworks capable of supporting genuine liberation struggles or retreat into abstract formulations that serve ruling-class interests through pseudo-radical inaction. The Trump test has exposed the bankruptcy of the second approach. The task now is building organizations capable of implementing the first.

Strategic Takeaway: Revolutionary organizations must understand that supporting concrete democratic struggles against immediate oppression strengthens rather than weakens international solidarity, requiring analytical frameworks sophisticated enough to distinguish genuine liberation movements from imperial proxies while maintaining principled independence from all great powers.

'International Socialism' Journal's Mistaken Illusion Of Chaos: Trump's Tariffs As Symptoms Of Systemic Decay

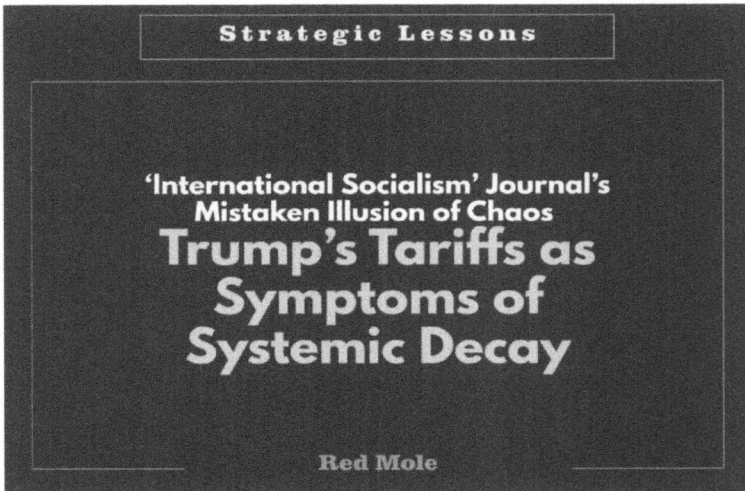

Strategic Lessons

'International Socialism' Journal's
Mistaken Illusion of Chaos
**Trump's Tariffs as
Symptoms of
Systemic Decay**

Red Mole

The lead article in the current International Socialism Journal, "Trump, tariffs and economic chaos" (by Rob Hoveman), correctly identifies the empirical chaos and the risk of economic instability, but its explanatory framework is constrained by viewing these outcomes largely as a consequence of political volatility and poor economic management. By focusing predominantly on the specific political actor and the immediate policy announcement, the analysis fails to articulate the deep, underlying material contradictions that compelled the US state to abandon neoliberal orthodoxy in the first place.

A Marxist analysis must reject this superficial focus on personality and policy. Tariffs are not the cause of chaos; they are desperate, incoherent symptoms of systemic decay. The failure to grasp the material roots of this decay—the structural crisis of capital, the constraints of finance, and the emergence of new accumulation regimes—means the analysis cannot provide meaningful strategic guidance.

The ISJ and Hoveman must be taken seriously As the theoretical journal that reflects the views of the Socialist Workers Party (SWP) in Britain and its International Socialist Tendency, it is among the most credible journals published by any Marxist tendency in English. Hoveman has been an SWP member for most of the last 40 years, playing a leading role in its work in the Socialist Alliance and Respect party. While Hoveman was not an SWP member for a while, following disagreements over his work for then-MP George Galloway, he remained within the SWP's broader intellectual and activist community, closely aligned with the SWP's politics. He is now again a member. He has continued to contribute articles to Socialist Worker, the party's newspaper, and has appeared as a speaker at the SWP's Marxism festivals, repeatedly in the last few years.

Trump as the motor force for tariffs

In his International Socialism article, Hoveman presents the April 2025 tariffs as primarily a manifestation of Trump's political rhetoric and personal economic strategy. He acknowledges the tariffs as a response to the "Make America Great Again" narrative, noting they found support among workers who felt left behind during the neoliberal era. Hoveman recognizes a broader context of US economic decline, particularly the hollowing out of the manufacturing base and the large balance of payments deficit, suggesting the tariffs are not entirely random but rooted in genuine economic concerns.

However, this article argues that Hoveman's analysis remains fundamentally descriptive, focusing more on Trump's individual agency than on the deeper structural dynamics of capitalism.

An Interjection: Have we misread Hoveman?

Rob disagrees with this article's assessment of the ISJ article. He thinks that anyone with that reading either misunderstood the article or didn't read it. You should read it yourself rather than take anyone's word for it.

If you read it, you'll read that Rob's account of Trump's tariffs vividly documents the immediate impacts—such as the sweeping 10 percent basic tariff and the quote from Paul Krugman describing it as the "greatest shock to international trade in world history." However, he falls short in fully connecting these actions to the broader systemic imperatives of global capitalism. Instead, his portrayal tends to frame the tariffs primarily as manifestations of chaotic political preferences and unpredictable policy decisions, rather than as strategically motivated responses grounded in the structural contradictions of capitalism.

Systemic Context of Trump's Tariffs

The 'Further reading' section at the end of this article include several sources, including analyses from CEPR and other economic think tanks, which agree that Trump's tariffs serve strategic geopolitical and economic objectives. They are part of a broader movement towards s-called "strategic capitalism," where state interventions aim to address perceived threats from China, reassert US industrial strength, and challenge the global dominance of the dollar. These policies are embedded in a geopolitical struggle over global economic influence, illustrating how tariffs are instruments in an overarching effort to recalibrate US imperialist power within the framework of international capitalist competition. [1]

The Structural Contradictions of Capitalism

These economic analyses highlight that such tariffs are responses to the systemic contradictions of contemporary capitalism—particularly the decline in profit rates, the hollowing out of manufacturing, and the structural imbalance in global trade. For instance, the rise of China as a manufacturing powerhouse and its integration into the global economy through WTO membership have challenged US dominance, prompting protective measures that ostensibly aim to "counter rip-offs" and unfair trade practices. These measures aim to defend national sovereignty and strategic interests but are also intrinsic responses to the crises of overaccumulation, declining profitability, and the global reorganization of production.[2]

Political Choices and Systemic Pressures

Hoveman's account, as reflected in the critique, appears to overlook the extent to which these tariffs are interwoven with the systemic imperatives of capitalism—namely, the need to restore profitability, reassert imperial dominance, and manage the contradictions between finance and production. Instead, his emphasis on the undeniable chaos and erratic nature of Trump's policies ignores the underlying logic that such interventions often emerge from systemic crises, rather than random political whims.

Recent Academic and Analytical Perspectives

Recent scholarly and policy analyses, including reports on the economic fallout of tariffs, emphasize their role within a strategic contest over trade dominance, global influence, and control of raw materials and high-tech sectors. These actions are coherent with the broader tendency of capitalism to resort to protectionism in times of crisis, underlining the connection between Trump's policies and the systemic contradictions of capitalism.[3]

I. The Structural Critique: Methodology and Theoretical Precision

The analysis of Trump's tariffs demands a methodological approach that transcends superficial political narratives. As our critique of Hoveman's article suggests, a truly revolutionary framework must penetrate the "concrete totality of capital" by exposing its inherent long-term contradictions.

LENS A: ERNEST MANDEL: LONG WAVES AND THE STRUCTURAL CRISIS OF CAPITAL

Ernest Mandel's theoretical contribution provides the foundational lens for understanding contemporary economic volatility. His theorization of long waves (Kondratiev cycles) reveals capitalism as a dynamic system characterized by structural transformations rather than linear progress. Key aspects of the Mandel framework include:

Long Wave Dynamics
- Capitalism oscillates between expansive (Phase A) and depressive (Phase B) periods
- The current epoch, initiated in the early 1970s, represents a prolonged Phase B of structural stagnation

- Stagflation emerges as the defining symptom: simultaneous inflation and economic stagnation

Tendency of the Rate of Profit to Fall (TRPF)
- The fundamental contradiction of capitalist accumulation
- As capitalists invest increasingly in technology (constant capital) relative to labor (variable capital), the overall rate of profit declines
- Protectionist measures like tariffs represent desperate attempts to secure valorization channels for overaccumulated capital

Objective Socialization vs. Private Appropriation
- A core tension: increasing social interconnectedness of labor contrasts with private ownership
- Technological advances create potential for collective productivity, yet remain constrained by capitalist property relations

LENS B: FRANCISCO LOUÇÃ: FINANCIAL HEGEMONY AND INSTITUTIONAL RIGIDITY
Francisco Louçã's analysis extends Mandel's framework by examining the institutional mechanisms of capitalist adaptation:

Depressive Long Wave Characteristics
- Incomplete realignment of social and economic institutions
- Neoliberal solutions as a response to structural crisis:
  - Liberalization of financial flows
  - Privatization
  - Precarization of labor
  - Globalization of markets

Fictitious Capital and Financial Accumulation
- Financial claims divorced from real productive capacity
- A "financial norm of minimum profitability" that filters out non-profitable projects
- Systematic generation of speculative booms leading to abrupt devaluations

LENS C. CÉDRIC DURAND: TECHNO-FEUDAL POWER AND ACCUMULATION REGIMES
Cédric Durand's framework illuminates the emerging structure of contemporary capitalism:

Neo-Industrial State
- State increasingly aligned with digital oligarchies

- Subsidization of platform monopolies
- Technological rivalry as a key mechanism of geo-economic conflict

Rent Extraction Structures

Shift from traditional profit generation to parasitic rent capture
Digital platforms as new sites of value extraction
Technological control as a primary mode of accumulation

Synthesis: A Dialectical Approach to Crisis

The integration of these frameworks reveals capitalism's current phase as characterized by:
- Declining productive investment
- Rising financial speculation
- Increasing state intervention to secure digital rent extraction
- Structural inability to resolve fundamental contradictions

Methodological Implications

This approach demands:
- Rejecting surface-level political analysis
- Understanding economic phenomena as manifestations of deeper structural dynamics
- Developing a revolutionary methodology that can comprehend capitalism's total movement

The tariffs are not chaos, but a symptomatic response to systemic contradictions—a desperate attempt to manage an increasingly unstable accumulation regime.

By adopting this rigorous theoretical framework, revolutionary movements can move beyond reactive struggles to develop a comprehensive strategy for systemic transformation.

Combining the Lenses: Tariffs as Systemic Symptomatology

MANDEL'S PERSPECTIVE: THE FALLING RATE OF PROFIT AS STRUCTURAL COMPULSION

From Mandel's long-wave analysis, the tariffs represent a classic manifestation of the Tendency of the Rate of Profit to Fall (TRPF). The US manufacturing base's hollowing out is not an aberration but a structural necessity of late capitalism. As technological investment increasingly replaces living labor, the fundamental value-generating mechanism of capitalism breaks down.

The 10% global tariff and punitive measures (up to 46% on countries like Vietnam) are not random policy choices but systematic attempts to:
- Artificially prop up domestic manufacturing
- Create protective barriers against international competition

- Secure valorization channels for overaccumulated capital

The tariffs reveal capitalism's inherent contradiction: the system must constantly generate new mechanisms of value extraction as its primary productive logic becomes increasingly unsustainable.

LOUÇÃ'S FINANCIAL HEGEMONY: FICTITIOUS CAPITAL'S DISCIPLINARY POWER

Through Francisco Louçã's lens, the tariffs expose the coercive power of fictitious capital. The bond market's immediate seven-day intervention demonstrates that political economic decisions are fundamentally constrained by financial accumulation regimes.

The tariffs represent an attempt to:

- Maintain creditor confidence
- Generate new financial speculation opportunities
- Create alternative valorization mechanisms when traditional productive investments fail

The financial norm of minimum profitability filters out less profitable projects, compelling increasingly desperate and volatile economic interventions.

DURAND'S TECHNO-FEUDAL INTERPRETATION: THE NEO-INDUSTRIAL STATE IN ACTION

Durand reveals the tariffs as a manifestation of the emerging techno-feudal power structure. This is not merely protectionism but a strategic reconfiguration of global technological and economic control.

Key dimensions include:

- Securing strategic technological assets (semiconductors, rare earth minerals)
- Restructuring global supply chains
- Aligning state power with digital oligarchies
- Creating new rent-extraction mechanisms through technological control

The tariffs represent a shift from traditional market competition to a more centralized, technologically mediated form of economic governance.

I'll craft a new section drawing directly from the Viento Sur article that can be integrated into the existing draft. Here's a proposed section:

The Factional Landscape of US Capital

Drawing on Cédric Durand and Benjamin Braun's analysis in Viento Sur, we can understand the tariffs as a complex negotiation between competing fractions of capital. Their article reveals a critical insight: Trump's economic strategy represents a precarious balancing act between multiple, often contradictory economic interests.

Competing Capital Factions

MAGA NATIONALIST FACTION

- Seeks to rebuild US manufacturing
- Advocates protectionist policies
- Supports restrictive immigration measures

PRIVATE FINANCIAL SECTOR

- Prioritizes tax privileges
- Demands systematic deregulation
- Seeks access to new investment pools (particularly 401(k) funds)

TECH OLIGARCHIES

- Desire global digital platform control
- Seek to maintain technological hegemony
- Increasingly aligned with state power

FOSSIL FUEL AND DEFENSE TECH COMPANIES

- Benefit from nationalist-militarist policies
- Support expanded state intervention in strategic sectors

The tariffs emerge not as a coherent strategy, but as a complex negotiation between these factions. Each group attempts to leverage Trump's political momentum to advance its specific economic interests, creating a volatile and potentially unstable economic configuration.

The Braudelian Twilight

Referencing historian Fernand Braudel's concept of imperial "autumn", Durand illuminates how these tariffs represent more than economic policy—they are symptomatic of a hegemonic power in systemic decline. The tariffs reveal a system frantically seeking to maintain its global economic position through increasingly desperate and incoherent interventions.

This fractured landscape exposes the fundamental contradictions of contemporary capitalism: the increasing tension between global financial flows, technological control, and traditional modes of industrial production. The revolutionary challenge is to understand these dynamics not as isolated phenomena, but as interconnected expressions of a system in profound structural crisis.

Systemic Contradictions Laid Bare

The tariffs thus reveal three fundamental systemic contradictions:
1. Productive Capacity vs. Accumulation Logic
   Capitalism's need for continuous expansion conflicts with its diminishing capacity to generate value through traditional productive mechanisms.
2. Financial Abstraction vs. Real Economic Needs
   The supremacy of fictitious capital creates increasingly volatile and disconnected economic interventions.
3. Technological Control vs. Global Labor Dynamics

The emergence of techno-feudal structures fundamentally transforms traditional relationships of production and exploitation.

Revolutionary Implications

These tariffs are not chaos, but a desperate institutional response to capitalism's structural crisis. They demonstrate the system's:

- Increasing irrationality
- Diminishing capacity for sustainable growth
- Fundamental inability to resolve its internal contradictions

The revolutionary task is to expose these systemic limitations, develop internationalist working-class strategies, and create alternative modes of economic organization that prioritize human needs over capital accumulation.

The tariffs thus become a critical diagnostic tool, revealing the deep, structural mutations of contemporary capitalism—a system frantically seeking survival mechanisms while simultaneously accelerating its own potential dissolution.

II. The Organizational Imperative: Concrete Strategic Guidance

A superficial analysis that focuses on the political surface is politically dangerous, as it risks reducing revolutionary struggle to "reformism from below" (fighting only for immediate wages), leading to a failure to articulate the necessary program of systemic rupture.

The structural analysis provides the necessary framework for strategic intervention:

1. TRANSITIONAL DEMANDS AND PROGRAMMATIC RUPTURE

Revolutionary organizations must adopt a strategy of transitional demands to prepare the working class for power. This movement requires confronting fundamental systemic failures rather than merely correcting inequities via fiscal redistribution, which is condemned to being a "labour of Sisyphus" within capitalism's limits.

The core objective is summarized as ensuring "common decency": assuring all individuals guaranteed employment and/or income, access to quality public services, and a decent planet.

A program for transformation must follow a systematic approach:

- Rupture:
  This involves taking immediate steps to protect against predictable retaliation and to build dual legitimacy. This includes establishing social legitimacy by prioritising lower incomes and minimum social standards.
- The Next Step Forward:
  The essential economic demands that articulate rupture include the reduction of working time and the State acting as employer of last resort. These necessary ruptures imply a degree of social confrontation that

reformist social-liberalism is unwilling to assume.
- Defining the Goal (Democratic Planning):
  The fundamental alternative to the chaos of market mechanisms is socialist planning. This planning must be democratic, pluralistic, and involve continuous worker control over production and resources, which is crucial for ferreting out unused production capacities. Planning must shift priorities away from market logic, for example, prioritising the building of schools and working-class housing over luxury flats, even if the former yields zero "profit". The ultimate aim is the withering-away of money economy, classes, and the state.

2. BUILDING THE REVOLUTIONARY VANGUARD

The victory of a revolution requires conscious preparation, including the development of experienced militants and a sound political program.
- The key task is to insert yourself in the service of the working class, not to adapt to the average level of consciousness, but to systematically prepare for the moment of crisis, which can and will break out in the next months and years in all of most of the important Western countries.
- Revolutionary cadre must build nuclei to make concrete propositions to show the workers and our allies how to make the next step forward beyond immediate demands.
- Revolutionary organizations must prioritise solving the central problems of the current period, otherwise they risk falling into sectarianism, where defending a single doctrinal point becomes a "shibboleth" and subordinates activity to that defence.

III. International Solidarity and Global Strategy

The structural crisis of capital is a global phenomenon, necessitating an internationalist response.

1. REJECTING NATIONAL RETREAT
- The US imperialist bourgeoisie cannot pursue world domination without assuming leadership of the entire capitalist world. The analysis in International Socialism must be critiqued for failing to provide an analysis of the world system that shows the interaction between the crises in the East and the West.
- Necessity of Global Strategy:
  Anti-capitalist forces must oppose the international counterrevolutionary strategy of Big Capital with a corresponding world-wide, global strategy.
- Utopian Nationalism:
  A case in point is the SWP's support for Brexit. It is totally utopian to believe one working class could meet the challenge by retreating into self-defence measures on a national scale. Measures like protectionism

risk offering an opportunity to the state to appear as the protector of both the bourgeoisie and workers of the same nation, diverting attention away from social conflict.

* Imperialism and Opportunism:
  The high monopoly profits secured by imperialist powers make it economically possible to bribe an upper strata of the proletariat, fostering opportunism and splitting the working-class movement. The fight against imperialism is a sham, as Lenin says, unless it is "inseparably bound up with the fight against opportunism".

2. THE GLOBAL REVOLUTIONARY PROCESS

The global class struggle must encompass the three sectors of the world revolution: the imperialist countries, the countries under bureaucratic dictatorships (Cuba, North Korea), and the developing countries.

The Permanent Revolution: The theory of permanent revolution argues that socialist revolutions are inevitable and unavoidable in backward countries if they are to save themselves from misery, ignorance, and backwardness. Only where capitalism has been overturned and the bourgeois state destroyed has there been a real agrarian revolution and subsequent economic growth (e.g., in the Soviet Union and China).

The International Imperative: The struggle for a Socialist World Federation is the central issue of our epoch. The internationalisation of capital compels the growing unity of action among workers worldwide to oppose multinational corporations. The International is our "real fatherland".

Conclusion: Synthesis of Strategic Insights

The episode of Trump's tariffs, far from being political chaos, confirms the deepening structural contradictions of late capitalism. The system is compelled by the crisis of overaccumulation to rely on a permanent arms economy (PAE) as "substitutive investment", while simultaneously facing rigid institutional constraints imposed by financial hegemony.

The practical conclusion for revolutionary movements is clear: the current conjuncture increases the volatility of the situation. The revolutionary task is to build a strong, internationalist alternative based on socialist planning and democratic rupture, preparing the working class to seize the opportunities presented by crisis and prevent the high social cost of capitalist adaptation. The focus must be on liberating the creativity that capital suffocates by offering a concrete program for "common decency".

FURTHER READING

https://www.riksbank.se/globalassets/media/rapporter/ppr/fordjupninga r/engelska/2024/241219/macroeconomic-effects-of-higher-us-import-tariffs-analysis-in-monetary-policy-report-december-2024.pdf

https://fiia.fi/en/publication/trumps-tariffs

https://www.europarl.europa.eu/RegData/etudes/IDAN/2025/764382/E CTI_IDA(2025)764382_EN.pdf

https://www.cepii.fr/PDF_PUB/pb/2024/pb2024-49.pdf

https://www.jpmorgan.com/insights/global-research/current-events/us-tariffs

https://www.cato.org/blog/trumps-state-capitalism-hybrid-between-socialism-capitalism-wont-make-america-great-again

https://www.claconnect.com/en/resources/articles/25/the-impact-of-trumps-tariffs-a-comprehensive-analysis

https://cepr.org/voxeu/columns/trumps-tariffs-fiscal-folly

https://www.ranenetwork.com/blog/the-visible-hand-trumps-interventionism-reshapes-american-capitalism

https://www.theatlantic.com/ideas/archive/2025/09/trump-economic-pain-strategy/684166/

https://www.cfr.org/trade-tariffs-and-trumponomics

https://www.theleftberlin.com/author/rob-hoveman/

https://www.sciencedirect.com/science/article/pii/S0165176525002174

https://arxiv.org/html/2506.00999v1

https://www.bbc.com/news/articles/cn85n2vg04go

https://prospect.org/economy/2025-10-20-state-or-just-trump-capitalism/

https://www.thenation.com/article/society/donald-trump-theory-of-politics-state/

Scottish Left Warns Corbyn's New Party: "No More Branch Officers" Why Your Party Must Choose Independence or Irrelevance

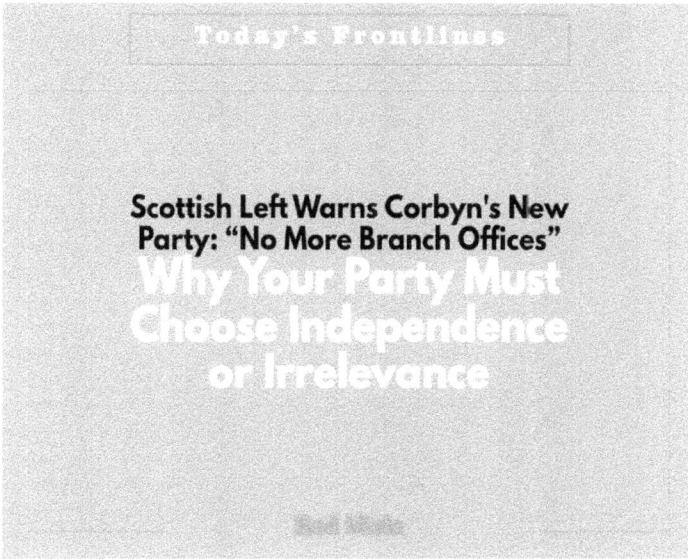

Jeremy Corbyn and Zarah Sultana's newly announced "Your Party" is already raising concerns among Scottish left activists who warn the venture could collapse before it starts if it continues ignoring the national question. The harsh reality? Scotland's left has watched this movie before – and it always ends in failure.

Bella Caledonia sums it up: "Limited consideration of Scotland has taken place in this attempt to get a left of Labour electoral challenge up and running," observes Democratic Left Scotland, while Richie Venton of the Scottish Socialist Party warns that "any new party that seeks to operate in Scotland must respect the right of the Scottish people to self-determination and must not be a mere branch office of a London-centric project."

This isn't just Scottish sensitivity – it's strategic necessity. The historical record is unforgiving: centralized left parties that ignore national questions don't just fail in Scotland, they fragment entirely. Spain's catastrophic left retreat in the 1990s offers a perfect case study of what happens when socialists dismiss plurinational realities.

The Spanish Warning: How Centralism Destroyed the Left

The Spanish Socialist Workers' Party (PSOE) once dominated the left. The left magazine Viento Sur describes its failures. By the 1990s, it had become a "neoliberal force with progressive trappings," transforming into what critics called a "party-cartel" that monopolized politics through state financing while abandoning its working-class identity. But PSOE's fatal error wasn't just embracing neoliberalism – it was promoting a divisive "theory of two national communities" that alienated Catalonia, the Basque Country, and Galicia.

In the Basque Country, PSOE manufactured a false division between communities, casting Basques as "bourgeois and racist" nationalists opposed to "working-class, socialist, and universalist" speakers of Castilian Spanish. This strategy poisoned dialogue and drove communities apart. This wasn't just bad politics – it was organizational suicide.

Izquierda Unida (IU), formed as a left alternative to PSOE, repeated the same mistakes. Despite its anti-capitalist rhetoric, IU struggled with a chronic inability to accept the plurinational reality of the Spanish state. Strong centralist currents within IU viewed national demands as "sectarian" or "right-wing," fatally undermining the party's ability to build genuine grassroots support in the Basque Country, Catalonia and Galicia.

The results were devastating. In Galicia, the rise of the Bloque Nacionalista Galego (BNG) captured the "vote of discontent" while IU's components struggled to reach even 3% of the vote. The lesson couldn't be clearer: Spain's alternative left faces a binary choice: either genuinely champion the distinct national identities and self-determination rights of its regions, or accept political marginalization and eventual collapse.

Scotland's Clear Message: Autonomy Works, Branch Offices Don't

Scottish left parties have learned this lesson the hard way. The most successful examples – the Scottish Socialist Party and Scottish Greens – operate as genuinely independent entities, not subordinate branches of UK-wide organizations.

The Scottish Greens emerged in 1990 when the former UK Green Party deliberately separated into two independent parties. Today, they're completely separate and unique with their own leaders, membership, and policies. Their strong support for Scottish independence isn't incidental – it's integral to their identity and success.

Similarly, the Scottish Socialist Party formed in 1998 from the Scottish Socialist Alliance, explicitly as a distinct Scottish entity. The SSP unequivocally supports independence, framing it through "internationalist rather than nationalist concerns" and advocating for a "Scottish socialist republic."

Contrast this with parties that maintained centralized structures. The Respect Party, "established in London" with no distinct Scottish presence, made virtually no impact north of the border and even lost supporters in England who opposed its organising north of the border. The pattern is clear: Scottish voters reject "branch office" politics.

Ross Greer, the Scottish Green MSP, put it bluntly: "The idea of a new London-based party trying to establish a 'branch office' in Scotland without a clear understanding of our distinct political context is deeply concerning."

WHY "YOUR PARTY" RISKS DISASTER

Troubling early indicators suggest "Your Party" risks repeating these historical errors. Scottish commentators describe the initial launch as "badly bungled and incoherent," with conflicting reports about organizational structure and minimal Scottish input.

Helena from 'No Justice' captures the frustration: Rolling out "Jeremy Corbyn as a 'left-leader' and harking back (uncritically) to how wonderful he was" isn't "serious politics." The party risks being dismissed as nostalgic English leftism that ignores Scottish political realities.

Most critically, "Your Party" has yet to clarify its position on Scottish self-determination—a silence that Scottish activists are already interpreting as indifference.. This isn't a minor oversight – it's a deal-breaker for many. As Ross Greer notes, "Scotland needs a strong, independent voice on the left, not another Westminster-controlled outfit."

The electoral arithmetic is brutal. Connor Beaton warns that attempting to contest Holyrood elections without broad engagement could "end up like RISE in 2016, winning a derisory share of the vote which then contributes to the whole project's collapse."

THE PLATFORM FOR SOCIALISM AND INDEPENDENCE

The good news is that Scottish socialists are already organizing to prevent this disaster. The recently launched Platform for Socialism and Independence brings together Aberdeen Marxist Caucus, the Republican Socialist Platform, Scottish Socialist Youth, and Socialists for Independence. It represents exactly the kind of proactive intervention needed. Rather than waiting for "Your Party" to impose a structure from London, these groups are engaging strategically while maintaining core principles around independence and Scottish autonomy.

The Path Forward: Embrace Plurinationalism

Jamie Driscoll, involved in "Your Party's" formation, seems to understand the stakes, emphasizing "significant autonomy in the nations and regions" and rejecting a "top-down London-run party." But good intentions aren't enough – organizational structure matters.

Based on successful precedents, "Your Party" needs to:

- Unequivocally support Scottish self-determination – not as a tactical position, but as a foundational principle. The Spanish experience shows that half-measures create "artificial barriers of incommunication."
- Foster genuine autonomy – Scottish and Welsh wings must have their own leadership, decision-making structures, and tailored political programmes. The Scottish Greens' model of formal separation or the SSP's autonomous development offer proven templates.
- Build grassroots power first – Instead of immediate Holyrood campaigns, focus on local organizing and council elections in 2027. This

allows time to develop genuine Scottish leadership and avoid the "excessive politicismo" that doomed Spain's IU.

- Engage existing Scottish movements – Work with independence campaigns, climate justice groups, Palestine solidarity, and other progressive forces rather than competing with them.

Learning from Failure in the Spanish State

The Spanish left's 1990s retreat wasn't inevitable – it resulted from strategic choices that prioritized institutional power over grassroots organizing and centralized control over plurinational democracy. These same pressures exist today.

"Your Party" can succeed, but only if it learns from these failures. The choice is stark: embrace genuine autonomy for Scotland and Wales, or watch another promising left initiative fragment on the rocks of unresolved national questions.

The Scottish left has been clear about what it needs. The question is whether Corbyn and Sultana are listening – or whether they're destined to repeat the mistakes that have buried left parties across Europe.

As Richie Venton warns: "We've seen countless attempts to build left-wing unity in Scotland only to see them fail because of a lack of understanding of the Scottish political landscape and the need for a genuinely independent Scottish socialist movement."

This is "Your Party's" moment of truth. The early warning signs are flashing red, but the fatal mistakes haven't been locked in yet. Corbyn and Sultana can still demonstrate they understand what every successful Scottish left party has learned: revolutionary democracy means unequivocally supporting self-determination. The choice is stark—act now to embrace genuine Scottish autonomy, or watch another promising left initiative fragment on familiar rocks.

FURTHER READING FROM SPAIN

To provide readers with background to the article "Spain's 1990s Left: Lessons for Scotland's Future," we recommend the following items in Viento Sur, the review published by the Fourth Internationalists in the Spanish state. Sadly, we have not been able to find English-language translations of these items.

• Issue 1. The introductory note for the "El desorden internacional" section in Viento Sur: This editorial outlines the section's purpose to feature "analysis and opinions on current international politics from left-wing people in other countries" and to address the "lack of bridges, of dialogue, that exists within the left internationally". This helps to set the stage for understanding the main article's

• Issue 3. The "Plural" section on national identity in Viento Sur: This section specifically focuses on "problems related to national identity" and presents "plural opinions" on this complex subject. Understanding these internal debates is crucial given that the "Spain's 1990s Left" article emphasizes the "national question" and the imperative for a genuinely emancipatory project to "unequivocally support self-determination and embrace the plurinational, plurilingual, and pluricultural nature of the state".

• Issue 4: Ralph Miliband, "La ideología socialdemócrata": This article, available in English at New Left Review, a review of Ludolfo Paramio's book, offers a critical perspective on the ideological justification of social-democratic identity and strategy. It is highly relevant for understanding the Spanish Socialist Workers' Party (PSOE)'s transition from a "reformist revolutionary" party to a "neoliberal force with progressive trappings", a central aspect of the crisis of the Spanish Left discussed in the main article.

• Issue 5. Alfonso Ortí's analyses of the PSOE and the post-Franco transition: Ortí provides a "historical and class interpretation" of the PSOE's evolution into a "social-technocracy" operating within the capitalist framework. His work helps to elucidate the PSOE's transformation into a "party-cártel" focused on governance rather than fundamental change, which is highlighted as a key lesson for the left in Scotland.

• Issue 5. "La reacción desde los movimientos" (on new social movements in the Spanish State): This piece describes the emergence and unique characteristics of new social movements in Spain, detailing how they differed from those in other Western countries. It provides essential context for the main article's call to move "Beyond Electoralism: Build Social Power," emphasizing that "electoral success is secondary to building deep roots in social movements" for true social transformation.emphasis on reasserting "Internationalism Against 'Nationalist' Economic Protectionism" as a vital step towards broader internationalist solidarity against global capitalism.

Building Left Counter-Power: How to Defeat Neoliberalism and Avoid Organizational Collapse

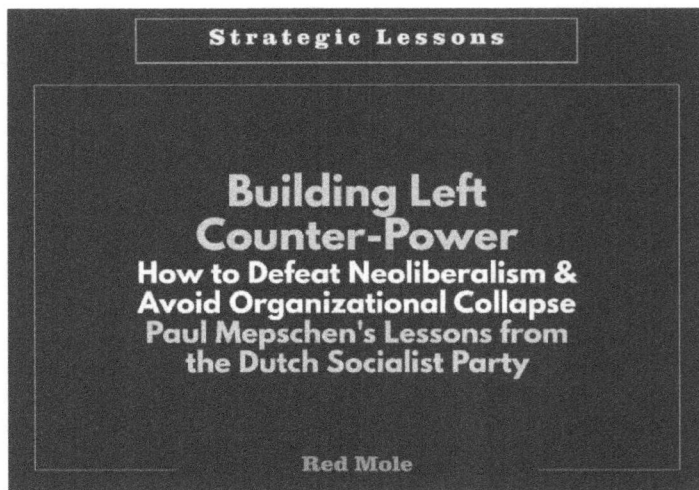

Strategic Lessons

Building Left
Counter-Power
How to Defeat Neoliberalism &
Avoid Organizational Collapse
Paul Mepschen's Lessons from
the Dutch Socialist Party

Red Mole

Paul Mepschen's Lessons from the Dutch Socialist Party

The most urgent challenge facing any burgeoning socialist alternative, whether in Britain, the United States, or elsewhere, is not merely confronting capital, but avoiding organizational collapse through ideological co-option or parliamentary drift. The decades-long triumph of neoliberalism has created a global crisis where traditional social-democratic parties surrender their principles, absorbing market ideology like a sponge. The resulting vacuum of representation demands a new revolutionary approach. The experience of the Dutch Socialist Party (SP), analyzed by revolutionary organizers like Paul Mepschen in the early 2000s, offers crucial lessons for contemporary movements worldwide. Mepschen, who died in November 2025, offered an analysis that is a powerful guide to those building class struggle movements today.

Paul Mepschen's Queer Politics: Beyond Tolerance to Liberation

To understand Paul Mepschen's strategic vision for the Dutch Socialist Party, we must begin with his most uncompromising ideological commitment: the refusal to accept mere tolerance as emancipation. This position was grounded not in academic queer theory, but in his lived experience as a Dutch gay man navigating Dutch society. Despite his Marxist analysis, Mepschen understood himself as embedded within his country's generation and culture; and he refused to allow that embeddedness to become an excuse for settling for second-class citizenship.

The distinction is critical: Mepschen rejected the liberal concept of acceptance and "tolerance," arguing instead for genuine sexual liberation:

"Tolerance is ideology; the struggle for sexual liberation is not about being tolerated!"

This position was not abstract moralizing. In Dutch society of the 2000s, tolerating gay people meant accepting their existence within strict, managed boundaries; visible, domesticated, but fundamentally subordinate. Mepschen rejected this framework entirely. The struggle was for actual freedom to live and love without subordination to heteronormative state structures or bourgeois "respectability." This meant fighting structural heteronormativity, not merely securing legal rights or social acceptance.

Against Culturalizing Poverty and Marginalization

Paul Mepschen's intellectual trajectory illuminates why the struggle against the "culturalization" of social problems is inseparable from revolutionary strategy. His doctoral research, "Everyday Autochthony: Difference, Discontent and the Politics of Home in Amsterdam" (2016), reveals the material foundation of his thinking. Through ethnographic research on working-class communities in Amsterdam's New West neighborhood, Mepschen demonstrated his deep capacity for understanding Dutch working people, not with contempt, but with genuine comprehension of how they navigated structural change and marginalization.

This is crucial because the dominant left tendency of his era was to attribute the drift toward racism, xenophobia, and right-wing populism to the "cultural deficiencies" of white working people. Mepschen rejected this analysis entirely. He acknowledged that working-class Dutch people harbored racist attitudes; this was undeniable. But he refused to ground this racism in some essential Dutch whiteness or cultural backwardness. Instead, he traced it to material causes: neoliberal policy, precarious employment, declining social services, and deliberate political manipulation by the bourgeoisie.

The stakes of this analysis were strategic: if racism flows from cultural deficiency, then the working class is an obstacle to liberation, and intellectuals must educate them into better values. If racism flows from structural marginalization under neoliberalism, then the working class is the potential social force for revolutionary transformation, precisely because they experience these contradictions most acutely. Mepschen chose the second path.

This commitment manifested in his concrete educational work. As he reflected:

"I teach in Rotterdam, at a vocational school in Rotterdam South. It is a school with struggling children with few prospects, largely but not exclusively immigrant. Children from the underclass. This is my ninth year. My profession is educator, much more than teacher."

This was not charity; it was class struggle. His work with young people navigating marginalization and precarity was rooted in the conviction that genuine opposition to neoliberalism must be grounded in combating its structural consequences, not in cultural nationalism or assimilationism.

Working-Class Anti-Neoliberalism as Strategic Foundation

These positions on queer liberation and against culturalization converge in Mepschen's core strategic insight: neoliberalism, not cultural deficiency, is the central explanation for the drift to the right and toward racism in contemporary society. This analysis unified his entire revolutionary project.

The Dutch context made this clear. The path of the Dutch Labour Party (PvdA) served as a universal cautionary tale. PvdA's conversion into a "social-neoliberal party" accelerated "the demolition of solidarity, the stripping down of social security." This betrayal created a "deep social crisis," providing fertile ground for both the extreme right (Fortuynism) and the anti-neoliberal SP.

Paul Mepschen, as a Fourth Internationalist and organizer then engaged within the SP, confirmed that the party grew precisely because it stood "as the voice of the opposition to neo-liberalism." The SP's strategic breakthrough came through its 2005 campaign for the mass "NO" vote against the proposed European Constitution, a referendum the party was instrumental in organizing.

That campaign proved transformative. The results were decisive: a "massive 'no' against the constitution" expressed the profound gap between political elites and ordinary people. The SP was, significantly, "the only left party which campaigned for the NO" against the proposed neoliberal treaty. The party's subsequent 2006 electoral breakthrough would mirror the composition of that 2005 "No" vote; proof that the party had successfully connected global ideological resistance to the daily needs and democratic anger of ordinary people.

This electoral growth, however, generated new dangers. And here Mepschen's integrated analysis becomes essential: the struggle against neoliberalism must simultaneously be a struggle against all forms of oppression: racism, heteronormativity, patriarchy. Without this integration, the anti-neoliberal movement fragments, and the far-right monopolizes opposition to liberal cosmopolitanism. Without this integration, queer and immigrant communities see themselves as having no stake in the anti-neoliberal project. The revolutionary alternative to neoliberalism must be a genuinely unifying project. Yet despite Mepschen and other left-wing activists' attempts to reverse this trajectory through the 2007 Congress debates, the SP ultimately failed these organizational tests. Yet despite Mepschen and other left-wing SP activists' attempts to institutionalize these reforms through the 2007 Congress debates, the SP would ultimately fail these tests.

The SP's Actual Trajectory: Why These Warnings Were Not Heeded

Despite the prescient warnings articulated at the 2007 Congress and the concrete structural proposals put forward by SP left-wingers, the party continued its trajectory toward parliamentary moderation and ideological compromise. The vulnerabilities Mepschen identified did not remain theoretical; they metastasized into permanent institutional features of the SP's functioning.

By 2024-2025, the situation had become untenable. The great majority of SP left-wingers, unable to reverse the party's rightward drift and unable to build the organizational counter-power Mepschen had advocated for, left the party. Paul Mepschen was among them. His final political statement, reflected in his last Facebook profile before his death in November 2025, called for a vote for BIJ1—an explicitly anti-racist, anti-capitalist, and internationalist political formation that represented a genuine break from the SP's compromises.

The tragedy is instructive: when revolutionary activists within a radical party fail to institutionalize the structural counterweights Mepschen advocated for before parliamentary power becomes entrenched, the party will inevitably succumb to the vulnerabilities he diagnosed. The SP's experience across two decades—from the promising radicalism of its 2005 European Constitution campaign to its recent decline—demonstrates that good intentions and revolutionary vision are necessary but insufficient without deliberate organizational architecture designed to resist the gravitational pull of parliamentarism.

Three Vulnerabilities Every Radical Party Faces

Yet even as the SP grew electorally, serious questions emerged about whether this success would destroy the very revolutionary character that made it attractive. For any new left party, the obstacles faced by the SP are not unique Dutch problems, but inherent vulnerabilities threatening every radical movement attempting to acquire power without sacrificing its revolutionary character.

VULNERABILITY 1: THE DISCONNECT BETWEEN MASS SUPPORT AND ORGANIZATIONAL POWER

Electoral success can mask underlying strategic weakness. Mepschen stressed that the foundation of a socialist alternative remains vulnerable when:

"The enormous problem the SP and the whole of the militant Left face is that the amount of electoral support for the party stands in no proportion to the power of the social movements and the political activity of the people."

A party can win millions of votes while lacking the organized capacity to transform society. Votes alone do not build power; organized movements do. This disconnect is the first warning sign that a radical party is becoming isolated from the struggles it claims to represent.

VULNERABILITY 2: PARLIAMENTARY CO-OPTION AND THE DRIFT TO MODERATION

The gravitational pull toward becoming a "normal" social-democratic party is a permanent internal threat. This phenomenon is characterized by the political weight of elected officials overpowering the activist base. As noted by SP activists and organizers:

"The problem is that in the SP the weight of the parliamentary group and the groups in city councils have become much greater in comparison with the weight of militants outside of such institutions."

This institutional drift, what Dutch organizers called "faction-centrism," risks abandoning the fight against "the neoliberal demolition" for the pursuit of consensus and parliamentary acceptability. It is not a flaw of individual leaders, but a structural dynamic inherent to parliamentarism itself.

VULNERABILITY 3: IDEOLOGICAL DRIFT AND FAILURE ON ANTI-OPPRESSION STRUGGLES

Radical movements often fail if they do not aggressively integrate all forms of liberation struggle, allowing opponents to successfully weaponize cultural and identity issues against them. Mepschen specifically critiqued the SP for needing "a clearer anti-racist profile" and failing to profile strongly enough on "feminist and LGBT themes." His opposition to tolerance ideology directly informed this organizational critique.

Why is this a class strategy vulnerability, not just an identity issue?

The neoliberal right weaponizes cultural nationalism precisely because the radical left abandons these struggles to focus narrowly on economic redistribution. When radical parties fail to lead anti-racist, feminist, and LGBT liberation fights, they cede these movements to liberal co-option or allow the far-right to dominate discourse. The result: working-class communities fragment along identity lines, preventing the unified class consciousness necessary for revolutionary transformation. Mepschen's insistence that the SP adopt a "clearer anti-racist profile" and stronger "feminist and LGBT themes" was not cultural distraction; it was essential class strategy.

The anti-neoliberal struggle must be inextricably linked to opposing assimilation and combating racism, or it will fail to unify the diverse working class against capital.

Three Strategic Directives for Organizational Survival

To prevent organizational collapse and maintain a revolutionary trajectory, a new left party, whether in Britain, emerging from DSA chapters in the United States, or developing within European radical movements, must adhere to these directives. These lessons were articulated by SP militants and organizers, most urgently in the debates preceding the party's 15th National Congress in November 2007, as the party grappled with the consequences of its own electoral growth.

DIRECTIVE I: PRIORITIZE THE UTOPIAN PROJECT AND OFFENSIVE ALTERNATIVES

The party must deliberately shift its focus from defense to offense. The goal is not merely to mitigate neoliberal attacks, but to propose a completely different society. Mepschen demanded that the party commit to an ambitious vision, arguing that the SP must win people

"for the utopian project that the struggle for a 21st century socialism is."

He explicitly warned against prioritizing short-term governance:

"The most important goal is not to make the SP governable for the Labour Party and Christian Democracy, but to build leftist counter-power and win as many people as possible for a real alternative to the neoliberal demolition."

This distinction is critical. A radical party that pursues government eligibility above all else will inevitably compromise its principles to achieve office. A radical party that prioritizes building counter-power and articulating socialist alternatives will maintain its revolutionary character even when winning elections.

The strategic lesson: Develop compelling, utopian, anti-capitalist political programs before you seek office. Do not wait until electoral success forces you to moderate.

DIRECTIVE II: INSTITUTIONALIZE ACTIVIST POWER TO COUNTER PARLIAMENTARY DOMINANCE

To prevent the inevitable drift toward parliamentary absorption, the party must create structural mechanisms that keep activist power above elected official power. Recognizing this threat, SP militants and activists proposed a concrete structural solution: mandatory member working groups and commissions.

At the SP's 15th National Congress in November 2007, activists including Leo de Kleijn articulated the crisis clearly: "The problem is that in the SP the weight of the parliamentary group and the groups in city councils have become much greater in comparison with the weight of militants outside of such institutions." In response, they proposed that party members should be able to "organize on the basis of their specific knowledge, activity or both" within thematic working groups covering union organizing, international solidarity, feminist activism, and LGBT liberation.

The strategic intention was explicit: these groups would "function as alternatives to the practice in the party that most of the development of ideas and views happens in and around the parliamentary group." They were designed to serve three critical functions:

1. **Counterweight:** To challenge the disproportionate political weight of elected officials over activist membership.
2. **Idea Development:** To ensure that socialist alternatives, policy innovation, and political programs originate from rank-and-file activists and organizers, not solely from parliamentary staff.
3. **Deep Rooting:** To strengthen the party's embeddedness in key social struggles, unions, anti-racist organizing, feminist movements, reinforcing identity as a movement against neoliberalism rather than merely a legislative body.

Tellingly, parliamentary representatives opposed these proposals, arguing that Tweede Kamerleden (national parliamentary members) already possessed "sufficient knowledge" of relevant themes, thus making working groups redundant. This defensive response itself revealed the power dynamic the militants were attempting to overcome: the parliamentary faction viewed grassroots organizing as competition rather than complementary.

The critical strategic lesson: SP militants identified the vulnerability and proposed structural solutions. Whether these solutions were ultimately implemented effectively remains an open question; but the diagnosis itself is definitive. Every radical party faces identical structural pressures toward faction-centrism unless it deliberately constructs counterweights.

Practical question for revolutionary organizers:

Does your organization have member working groups functioning as genuine counterweight to elected officials? If not, you face the identical vulnerability that SP activists sought to overcome, and you need to act before parliamentary weight becomes insurmountable.

DIRECTIVE III: FIGHT FOR RADICAL PLURALISM AND REJECT ASSIMILATION

A socialist movement must be "as diverse as they come." This means actively integrating the struggles of marginalized communities, recognizing that "Diversity is one of the core elements of modern society." The party must take a clear stand "on the side of immigrants" and reject nationalist assimilation politics, which criminalize the vulnerable. Instead of seeking conformity, the party must fight for genuine autonomy: the right to choose and live freely on matters of sexuality and life, alongside the right to decent work and guaranteed income.

The objective is a "pluralistic, democratic, feminist, anti-racist and internationalist system of norms and values"; one that unites diverse working-class struggles under a common banner of structural transformation, not liberal tolerance.

The Test for Revolutionary Organizations

The question for revolutionary organizers today is not whether your organization will face these three vulnerabilities; you will. The question is whether you are structurally prepared to resist them.

The Dutch Socialist Party's experience at its 2007 Congress provides a definitive diagnosis: Even as the party won millions of votes following its successful 2005 European Constitution campaign, its own activists recognized that parliamentary power was overwhelming grassroots organizing. They identified the mechanism (faction-centrism) and proposed solutions (member working groups organized by theme and activity). Yet the parliamentary faction itself resisted these proposals, arguing that elected officials already possessed sufficient knowledge.

This resistance proves the point: the drift toward parliamentarism is not accidental, but structurally reinforced. Elected officials naturally defend their accumulated power against grassroots counterweights. Revolutionary organizations must anticipate this resistance and implement structural solutions before the parliamentary faction becomes powerful enough to block them.

Ask yourselves:

- Have you built member working groups as a counterweight to elected officials, or are you waiting until it's too late?
- Have you articulated an offensive socialist alternative, not just defensive resistance to neoliberal attacks?
- Have you made anti-racism and anti-imperialist solidarity non-negotiable organizational identity, not optional commitments?

For British activists building new left formations, American DSA chapters winning city council seats, or European radical parties managing governments, the Dutch Socialist Party's experience provides a tested diagnostic framework. The vulnerabilities are universal. The structural dynamics are predictable. The window for implementing counterweights is narrower than you think. Whether your revolutionary movement survives electoral success depends on whether you implement these directives now, before parliamentary weight threatens your revolutionary character.

Key articles by Paul Mepschen in Grenzeloos

Paul's articles for Grenzeloos are collected here:
https://www.grenzeloos.org/users/paul-mepschen

DE LINKSE TEGENMACHT VERSTERKEN

Strengthening Left Opposition to Neoliberalism in the SP
14.11.2007

This *Grenzeloos* article directly addresses the core organizational threats (Vulnerabilities 1 & 2) by arguing that the SP's mass support is disproportionate to the power of social movements. It explicitly proposes the structural solution advocated in Directive II: establishing thematic working groups as a "counterweight" to prevent ideas from being dominated by the parliamentary faction ("faction-centrism").

TEGEN TOLERANTIE

Against Tolerance: An Ideological Critique
01.06.2009

This *Grenzeloos* article provides the ideological foundation for Vulnerability 3 (Ideological Drift) and Directive III (Radical Pluralism). It asserts that the concept of tolerance is an ideology that mystifies real power struggles, demanding instead a fight against structural heteronormativity and a convergence of anti-racist and queer struggles.

EMANCIPATIE EN INTEGRATIE KUNNEN NIET ZONDER KLASSENSTRIJD

Class Struggle, Emancipation, and Integration Cannot Do Without Class Struggle

29.11.2008

Co-authored by Leo de Kleijn and Paul Mepschen,

This *Grenzeloos* article supports the strategic analysis that the marginalisation of migrant groups is a direct result of neoliberal policy, not cultural failure. It reinforces the claim that a "radical break with neoliberal policy is needed", arguing that anti-oppression struggles (Directive III) must be inextricably linked to class politics.

HET MOET EN KAN ANDERS

A Progressive Alternative to Dutch Neoliberalism

24.09.2005

This *Grenzeloos* article reinforces the context of the "Strategic Crisis" (PvdA betrayal) by detailing how the PvdA absorbed neoliberal ideology during the Kok cabinets. It directly supports Directive I (Prioritize the Utopian Project) by calling for focusing on building social movements and proposing radical, offensive alternatives such as work time reduction and wealth redistribution.

NEE TEGEN DIT EUROPA, REFERENDUM NU!

No to This Europe, Referendum Now!

26.09.2007

This *Grenzeloos* article documents the crucial 2005 "NO" vote against the EU Constitution, which the blueprint identifies as the turning point that confirmed the profound gap between elites and ordinary people and validated the SP's anti-neoliberal strategy. It showcases the PvdA leadership's commitment to the neoliberal project despite opposition from its base.

HOMO VOOR DE KLAS

A Gay Teacher in Rotterdam South

25.01.2006

This *Grenzeloos* article details Mepschen's experience as an educator working with struggling, mostly immigrant, children in Rotterdam South, underscoring the need for political opposition to be rooted in combating structural marginalization, not just parliamentary maneuvering.

What Is The True Revolutionary Tradition? Can Socialists Vote For France's NFP?

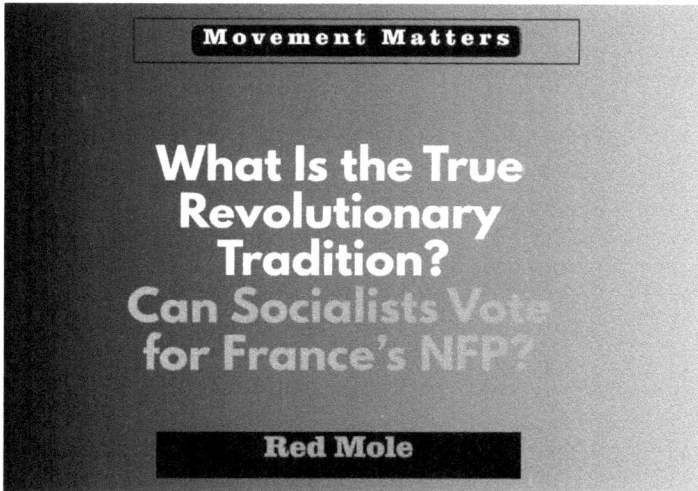

The 2022 fracturing of France's Nouveau Parti Anticapitaliste (NPA) into two distinct currents—NPA-Anticapitalistes (NPA-A) and NPA-Révolutionnaires (NPA-R)—has crystallized a fundamental debate that extends far beyond French borders. At its heart lies a question that has plagued revolutionary socialists for over a century: what constitutes authentic revolutionary practice, and can principled socialists participate in broader electoral alliances without betraying their core mission?

The split within the NPA, triggered largely by disagreements over participation in united fronts like La France Insoumise (LFI) and the Nouveau Front Populaire (NFP), represents more than organizational infighting. It embodies an enduring tension between "open" and "closed" conceptions of revolutionary party building—a tension that reveals competing interpretations of the revolutionary tradition itself.

The "Open" Path: Strategic Flexibility Within Revolutionary Principles

NPA-Anticapitalistes maintains an "open" approach, consistent with the legacy of the Ligue Communiste Révolutionnaire (LCR), prioritizing broad anti-capitalist unity and tactical flexibility, notably seen in their participation in the Nouveau Front Populaire (NFP). For Philippe Poutou and other NPA-A leaders, joining the NFP represents not electoral opportunism but a strategic vision to influence and ensure the left "dares to go on the offensive again" and "dares to assert itself as radical".

This approach finds deep theoretical grounding in the classical revolutionary tradition. The united front tactic emerged from the 3rd Comintern

Congress in 1921, recognizing the strategic necessity of engaging with the masses, even when they held illusions in reformist parties. Lenin himself actively opposed "left communists" who rejected such engagement, defending participation in bourgeois parliaments and emphasizing that revolutionaries should address the needs of the masses by taking "each need of the masses as a starting point for a revolutionary struggle".

The NFP differs qualitatively from the Popular Fronts that Trotsky opposed. The key difference is the NFP's exclusion of a major traditional bourgeois party, unlike the Popular Front of the 1930s which included the liberal Radical party. This distinction allows NPA-A to defend their participation as consistent with Trotskyist principles while avoiding the class-collaborationist trap that historically compromised Popular Front strategies.

François Sabado, a historical leader of the LCR/NPA, viewed the Nupes (a predecessor to NFP) as "politically positive", indicating a willingness for the NPA to engage in unity and dialogue with broader left forces while maintaining an independent anti-capitalist pole. This emphasis on both engagement and preservation of core principles represents a sophisticated understanding of how revolutionary forces can operate within broader formations without losing their distinctive identity.

Daniel Bensaïd's concept of "fertilizing the united front with revolutionary content" provides the theoretical framework for this strategy. Rather than passive participation, the goal is to inject revolutionary content into broader political struggles, using alliance platforms to advance anti-capitalist consciousness while maintaining clear programmatic independence.

The "Closed" Response: Independence as Revolutionary Necessity

NPA-Révolutionnaires gravitates towards a fundamentally different model, viewing broad alliances as "preparing new political traps for the workers". This stance draws strength from a rigorous analysis of twentieth-century history, particularly the Mitterrand administration of 1981, which their analysis suggests ultimately contributed to disorienting the working class, leading a significant portion of workers and youth, disillusioned by perceived betrayals, to turn to the Front National.

For NPA-R, this historical lesson provides the analytical framework for understanding contemporary dangers. The Mitterrand government's trajectory from socialist promises to neoliberal implementation demonstrates the concrete material consequences of left participation in bourgeois governance. From this perspective, the NFP represents not an opportunity but a repetition of historical patterns that inevitably end in the demoralization of revolutionary forces and the strengthening of reaction.

NPA-R frames the 2022 split as an "opportunity" to build a genuinely revolutionary, communist, and internationalist party, aiming for a "fusion" of militant experiences based on the centrality of the working class, with an objective for "our class to take the lead in mobilisations against oppressions", while also maintaining strict independence from the institutional left. Their approach emphasizes building a "cadre party" with highly trained militants, with a strong focus on workplace implantation.

This model finds theoretical support in Lutte Ouvrière's consistent practice of maintaining revolutionary independence. LO has systematically criticized other left groups for perceived compromises with "imperialism" and steadfastly asserts the working class as the sole, central force for revolution, maintaining focus on direct worker engagement rather than electoral combinations that dilute revolutionary clarity.

NPA-R's Criticisms and NPA-A's Robust Counter-Arguments

THE CHARGE OF "ELECTORAL CRETINISM"

NPA-R's Position: From NPA-R's perspective, participation in the NFP represents a classic case of "parliamentary cretinism"—the illusion that revolutionary goals can be advanced through participation in bourgeois electoral processes. They argue that the French state remains fundamentally bourgeois regardless of electoral outcomes, and participation implicitly accepts the legitimacy of bourgeois democratic institutions.

NPA-A's Response: This critique fundamentally misunderstands both the nature of the united front tactic and the concrete political situation in France. NPA-A does not harbor illusions about transforming the bourgeois state through electoral means. Rather, they recognize that mass consciousness develops through struggle, and the NFP provides a platform for advancing anti-capitalist ideas to audiences far broader than any revolutionary organization could reach independently.

Lenin's defense of participating in bourgeois parliaments was not based on illusions about parliamentary transformation but on the recognition that revolutionaries must engage where the masses are found. The NFP allows NPA-A to present anti-capitalist alternatives within a context where millions of people are already engaged, rather than preaching to the converted in sectarian isolation.

Moreover, the historical parallel to the Mitterrand government is fundamentally flawed. Mitterrand represented a traditional social-democratic party seeking governmental power within existing institutions. The NFP, by contrast, explicitly excludes bourgeois parties and represents a defensive alliance against the far-right rather than a governmental coalition seeking to manage capitalism.

THE QUESTION OF CLASS NATURE AND COMPROMISE

NPA-R's Position: Once committed to electoral success within the NFP, revolutionary forces inevitably face pressure to moderate their positions to maintain coalition unity. This dynamic leads to the progressive abandonment of revolutionary demands in favor of "realistic" reforms that pose no fundamental challenge to capitalist relations.

NPA-A's Response: This mechanistic understanding of political dynamics ignores the possibility of revolutionary leadership within broader formations. The experience of the LCR within various alliance structures demonstrates that principled revolutionaries can maintain their political independence while contributing to broader struggles.

The key lies in entering such alliances with clear programmatic demands and the willingness to break when fundamental principles are compromised. NPA-A maintains its organizational independence, continues to advance anti-capitalist positions, and reserves the right to criticize alliance partners when necessary. This is precisely what Lenin meant by "fertilizing" broader formations with revolutionary content.

Furthermore, the alternative proposed by NPA-R—pure organizational independence—has historically led to sectarian isolation that serves the bourgeoisie's interests by keeping revolutionary forces marginal and irrelevant to mass struggles. The Spanish experience provides a cautionary example: the failure of the left to address national questions and engage with broader social movements led to its marginalization and ultimate irrelevance.

HISTORICAL PRECEDENT AND THE MITTERRAND LEGACY

NPA-R's Position: The Mitterrand experience provides the most relevant case study: a left government that began with radical promises and ended by implementing austerity policies indistinguishable from those of the right. This demonstrates the systematic nature of reformist betrayal rather than individual moral failings.

NPA-A's Response: While the Mitterrand experience offers important lessons, drawing direct parallels to the NFP reveals a fundamental analytical error. Mitterrand represented a social-democratic party that explicitly sought governmental power within existing capitalist frameworks. The Socialist Party entered government with the intention of managing capitalism more humanely, not transforming it fundamentally.

The NFP, by contrast, represents a defensive alliance against fascist threats rather than a governmental project. Its formation responds to the immediate danger posed by the far-right, not the ambition to govern within capitalist parameters. Historical analysis must account for these concrete differences rather than applying mechanical formulas.

Moreover, the Mitterrand experience actually supports the necessity of revolutionary presence within broader formations. The absence of strong revolutionary voices within the Socialist Party contributed to its rightward drift. Revolutionary participation in broader alliances, with clear programmatic independence, can help prevent such trajectories by maintaining pressure for genuine anti-capitalist positions.

THE ILLUSION OF INFLUENCE

NPA-R's Position: NPA-A's claim that they can "influence" figures like Mélenchon fundamentally reverses the actual direction of influence. In practice, participation in such formations leads to the moderation of revolutionary forces rather than the radicalization of reformist ones.

NPA-A's Response: This argument reflects a profound misunderstanding of how political consciousness develops and how revolutionary organizations can effectively intervene in mass struggles. The assumption that revolutionaries are inevitably corrupted by contact with broader movements reveals a mechanical view of political development that has no basis in historical experience.

The LCR's historical engagement with diverse movements—student struggles, anti-racist campaigns, environmental activism—demonstrates that principled revolutionary organizations can maintain their identity while contributing to broader social struggles. The key lies in approaching such engagements with clear principles and the organizational capacity to maintain independence.

Furthermore, influence operates in multiple directions simultaneously. While revolutionaries must guard against accommodation pressures, their participation also creates opportunities to expose the limitations of reformist politics and present genuine alternatives. The crisis of traditional social democracy creates space for revolutionary ideas that would not exist in periods of reformist stability.

Contemporary examples support this analysis. In several European countries, revolutionary organizations have successfully used broader alliance platforms to advance anti-capitalist ideas and build their own organizational capacity. The mechanical assumption that participation inevitably leads to corruption ignores the possibility of skillful revolutionary leadership.

Beyond "Economism": NPA-A's Integrated Approach to Social Struggle
THE CRITIQUE OF WORKING-CLASS CENTRALITY

NPA-R's Position: While acknowledging various forms of oppression, NPA-R maintains that the industrial working class remains the only social force capable of fundamentally transforming capitalist society. The expansion of revolutionary politics beyond traditional class lines risks fragmenting struggle into competing identity-based movements that can be easily co-opted.

NPA-A's Response: This position, while claiming to avoid economism, actually reproduces its essential errors by maintaining a hierarchical view of social struggles that subordinates other forms of oppression to traditional working-class concerns. Lenin's critique of economism in "What Is To Be Done?" emphasized that Marxists must "understand all social contradictions and tendencies," not reduce them to a single primary contradiction.

The contemporary working class includes women, racial minorities, LGBTQ+ individuals, immigrants, and others who face multiple forms of oppression. A revolutionary strategy that fails to address these specific oppressions cannot effectively unite the working class, let alone lead it to victory. The apparent unity achieved by ignoring such differences is actually a false unity that reproduces existing hierarchies and exclusions.

The LCR's historical critique of Lutte Ouvrière's economism remains relevant: reducing revolutionary politics to "propaganda in the working class and intervention in economic struggles" ignores the complex reality of how oppression operates in contemporary capitalism. Effective revolutionary strategy must address racism, sexism, environmental destruction, and other forms of oppression as integral components of capitalist domination, not secondary issues to be addressed after the primary class struggle is resolved.

GRAMSCI AND EXTENDED REVOLUTIONARY AGENCY

NPA-R's Position: The emphasis on "intersectionality" and multiple oppressions, however valid sociologically, can undermine the strategic focus necessary for revolutionary success by fragmenting unified class struggle.

NPA-A's Response: This critique reveals a fundamental misunderstanding of both Gramscian theory and contemporary social reality. Gramsci's insights into hegemony and the expanded role of civil society in maintaining capitalist rule have become more relevant, not less, as capitalism has developed sophisticated mechanisms for incorporating and neutralizing opposition.

The integration of diverse social struggles does not fragment revolutionary potential but recognizes that capitalism operates through multiple systems of oppression that must be challenged simultaneously. Women's liberation, anti-racism, environmental justice, and LGBTQ+ rights are not distractions from class struggle but integral components of building the broadest possible coalition against capitalist domination.

Historical examples support this integrated approach. The most successful revolutionary movements have consistently linked class struggle to broader social questions. The Russian Revolution succeeded partly because the Bolsheviks addressed national questions and peasant concerns, not merely industrial worker demands. The Cuban Revolution integrated anti-imperialism with social transformation. Contemporary movements like those in Latin America demonstrate how linking class struggle to indigenous rights, environmental justice, and gender equality can build powerful anti-capitalist coalitions.

THE QUESTION OF AUTONOMOUS ORGANIZATION

NPA-R's Position: Rather than rejecting struggles against specific oppressions, NPA-R supports autonomous organization of oppressed groups while maintaining that such struggles achieve revolutionary potential only when linked to broader working-class struggle against capitalist exploitation.

NPA-A's Response: While this position appears more sophisticated than crude economism, it maintains the same essential hierarchy by insisting that working-class struggle remains primary and other struggles achieve significance only through their connection to it. This approach fails to recognize that different forms of oppression have their own dynamics and require autonomous development.

The historical experience of women's movements, anti-racist struggles, and other liberation movements demonstrates that autonomous organization often develops the most radical critiques of existing society. The slogan "the personal is political" emerged from autonomous feminist organizing and revealed how capitalism operates through the family, sexuality, and other spheres traditionally considered "private."

Rather than subordinating these movements to a predetermined working-class agenda, revolutionary strategy should recognize their autonomous development while seeking points of convergence and mutual support. The goal is not to absorb other movements into a working-class framework but to build solidarity between different struggles while maintaining respect for their specific dynamics and demands.

International Dimensions: Learning from Global Experience
THE EUROPEAN CONTEXT AND STRUCTURAL CONSTRAINTS

NPA-R's Position: The repeated failure of left governments across Europe—from SYRIZA in Greece to PSOE in Spain—demonstrates the systemic nature of the problem. European Union frameworks, NATO membership, and integration into global capitalism create structural constraints that make genuinely left policies impossible within existing state frameworks.

NPA-A's Response: While the SYRIZA experience offers important lessons, drawing mechanical conclusions from it misunderstands both the specific Greek context and the broader possibilities for revolutionary intervention. SYRIZA's failures resulted partly from its lack of revolutionary preparation and its illusions about managing capitalism more humanely. These failures do not invalidate all forms of alliance politics but rather highlight the necessity of revolutionary leadership within broader formations.

The European context does create structural constraints, but these constraints affect revolutionary organizations regardless of their tactical choices. Pure independence does not exempt revolutionary organizations from capitalist pressure; it simply ensures they face such pressure from a position of isolation and weakness.

More importantly, the crisis of European social democracy creates opportunities for revolutionary intervention that did not exist during periods of reformist stability. The collapse of traditional center-left parties opens space for genuine alternatives, but this space can be occupied either by revolutionary forces or by new varieties of reformism. Revolutionary participation in broader formations, with clear programmatic independence, can help ensure that this space is filled by genuine anti-capitalist alternatives.

CONTEMPORARY ANTI-FASCIST STRUGGLE

NPA-R's Position: The growth of far-right movements creates pressure for broad anti-fascist coalitions. However, the historical record suggests that such coalitions often strengthen rather than weaken fascist forces by demonstrating the bankruptcy of liberal democracy and the incapacity of the left to offer genuine alternatives.

NPA-A's Response: This analysis, while containing elements of truth, fundamentally misunderstands both the nature of contemporary fascist threats and the requirements of effective anti-fascist strategy. The growth of far-right movements results from the crisis of neoliberalism and the failure of traditional politics to address mass suffering. Under these conditions, revolutionary isolation serves fascist interests by leaving the field open to demagogic appeals.

Effective anti-fascist strategy requires building the broadest possible coalition while maintaining revolutionary independence within it. The NFP represents precisely this type of formation: a broad alliance that excludes bourgeois parties while bringing together various left forces against the far-right threat.

Historical analysis supports this approach. Fascism was defeated in the 1930s and 1940s through broad coalitions that included revolutionary forces maintaining their independence. Contemporary examples from countries like Germany demonstrate how revolutionary participation in anti-fascist coalitions can build organizational capacity while contributing to broader resistance.

The alternative proposed by NPA-R—building revolutionary capacity in isolation while fascist forces grow—historically leads to revolutionary organizations being crushed before they can become effective. The German experience provides a cautionary example of how sectarian independence in the face of fascist threats can lead to disaster for the entire working-class movement.

Responding to Charges of Opportunism

THE QUESTION OF PRINCIPLED VS. UNPRINCIPLED UNITY

NPA-R's Position: True unity must be based on shared revolutionary objectives rather than tactical convenience. The unity represented by the NFP is necessarily superficial because it papers over fundamental disagreements about objectives and methods.

NPA-A's Response: This position reveals a mechanical understanding of how political unity develops and how revolutionary consciousness emerges through struggle. Perfect programmatic agreement is not a prerequisite for tactical cooperation; indeed, such agreement is often the result of common struggle rather than its precondition.

The NFP brings together forces that share opposition to far-right reaction and commitment to defending democratic rights, even while maintaining different views about ultimate objectives. This provides a foundation for common action while creating opportunities for revolutionaries to demonstrate the superiority of their analysis and program through practice.

Lenin's approach to the united front emphasized that revolutionaries should cooperate with other forces around specific demands while maintaining the right to criticize their allies and present alternative solutions. This approach allows revolutionary organizations to build influence while contributing to immediate struggles that matter to working people.

THE LONG-TERM VS. SHORT-TERM PERSPECTIVE

NPA-R's Position: Revolutionary strategy requires a long-term perspective focused on building capacity for fundamental transformation rather than achieving short-term electoral gains that ultimately strengthen bourgeois institutions.

NPA-A's Response: This false counterposition between long-term strategy and immediate intervention misunderstands how revolutionary capacity is actually built. Revolutionary organizations develop through engagement with real struggles, not through abstract preparation for future opportunities.

The NFP provides immediate opportunities to resist far-right advancement while building revolutionary capacity through practical intervention. Participating revolutionaries gain experience in mass struggle, develop their analytical capacity through engagement with concrete political questions, and build relationships with broader layers of activists who may be recruited to revolutionary positions.

Historical examples demonstrate that successful revolutionary organizations have consistently combined long-term strategic thinking with tactical flexibility and willingness to engage in immediate struggles. The Bolsheviks' success resulted partly from their ability to intervene effectively in immediate political crises while maintaining their revolutionary objectives.

The sectarian alternative—building revolutionary capacity in isolation from mass struggles—historically leads to revolutionary organizations becoming irrelevant talking shops rather than effective interventions in real political developments.

The Revolutionary Tradition and Contemporary Application
INTERPRETING CLASSICAL SOURCES

The debate over NFP participation ultimately reflects different interpretations of the revolutionary tradition, particularly the works of Lenin and Trotsky. Both sides claim fidelity to classical sources while reaching opposite conclusions about contemporary tactical questions.

The historical development of the united front tactic provides the strongest support for NPA-A's position. Lenin's struggles against "left communism" and his defense of tactical flexibility established principles that remain relevant to contemporary conditions. The united front tactic emerged precisely to address situations where revolutionary organizations needed to engage with broader forces while maintaining their independence.

Trotsky's opposition to Popular Fronts was based on their inclusion of bourgeois parties, not on opposition to all forms of alliance politics. The NFP's exclusion of bourgeois parties places it qualitatively in a different category from the formations Trotsky opposed. Contemporary application of Trotskyist principles must account for concrete differences rather than applying mechanical formulas.

LEARNING FROM HISTORICAL EXPERIENCE

The historical record of revolutionary movements demonstrates the superiority of tactical flexibility over sectarian purity. The most successful revolutionary movements have consistently combined principled commitment to revolutionary objectives with willingness to engage in immediate struggles and form tactical alliances with other forces.

The Bolsheviks' success resulted partly from their ability to adapt their tactics to changing conditions while maintaining their strategic objectives. Lenin's April Theses represented a tactical shift rather than abandonment of revolutionary principles. Similarly, contemporary revolutionaries must adapt their tactics to current conditions while maintaining their commitment to fundamental transformation.

The 1971 Protocol of Agreement between the Ligue Communiste and Lutte Ouvrière outlined a shared theoretical basis rooted in the principles of Lenin, Trotsky, and the Fourth International, with the unified organisation explicitly intended to be the French section of the Fourth International. The protocol detailed specific conditions for unity, which included expectations for LO to overcome its perceived economism, engage across all spheres of class struggle, and accept democratic centralism within the unified organisation. This historical example demonstrates that even seemingly rigid positions can exhibit conditional flexibility when fundamental ideological differences can be addressed.

The historical failures of sectarian organizations provide equally important lessons. The various "pure" revolutionary groups that maintained isolation from mass struggles consistently failed to build significant influence or contribute to revolutionary advancement. Purity without influence serves no revolutionary purpose.

Building Revolutionary Capacity Through Engagement
THE QUESTION OF MASS WORK

Effective revolutionary strategy requires sustained engagement with mass struggles rather than isolation in pure organizational forms. The NFP provides opportunities for such engagement that would not exist for isolated revolutionary organizations.

Revolutionary capacity develops through practice rather than abstract study. Participating in the NFP allows revolutionaries to test their analysis against reality, develop their tactical skills through engagement with complex political situations, and build relationships with broader layers of activists and workers.

The alternative approach—building revolutionary capacity in isolation—historically leads to revolutionary organizations developing incorrect analyses, poor tactical judgment, and inability to relate to mass consciousness. Such organizations may maintain theoretical purity but lose the capacity for effective intervention.

ORGANIZATIONAL INDEPENDENCE WITHIN BROADER FORMATIONS

The key to successful revolutionary participation in broader formations lies in maintaining organizational independence while contributing to common struggles. This requires clear principles, strong internal democracy, and willingness to break with allies when fundamental issues arise.

NPA-A's approach demonstrates how revolutionary organizations can maintain their identity while participating in broader formations. They continue to advance anti-capitalist positions, maintain their organizational structure, and reserve the right to criticize alliance partners when necessary.

This model has historical precedent in the LCR's successful engagement with diverse movements over several decades. The LCR maintained its revolutionary identity while contributing to student struggles, anti-racist campaigns, environmental movements, and other social struggles that built broader consciousness and organizational capacity.

Contemporary Challenges and Strategic Implications

The current period presents specific challenges that affect strategic calculations about alliance politics. Contemporary debates, such as those surrounding the war in Ukraine, serve as compelling case studies illustrating divergences in united front and anti-imperialist positions. NPA-A's former platform C criticized NPA-R for its "perceived lack of explicit support for resistance in Palestine and Ukraine", while LO maintained a strong anti-imperialist line opposing support for any imperialist side. These debates underscore how theoretical differences regarding imperialism and alliances translate into conflicting policy positions on complex international issues.

The NFP debate also reflects the broader crisis of traditional social democratic parties, which have largely abandoned even rhetorical commitment to working-class interests, creating space for new formations. However, this space can be filled either by genuine revolutionary alternatives or by new varieties of left reformism that ultimately serve similar functions.

The growth of far-right movements creates additional pressure for broad anti-fascist coalitions. The environmental crisis requires urgent action that appears to demand broad coalitions. However, meaningful environmental action requires challenging capitalist growth imperatives, which broad coalitions systematically avoid in favor of technological and market-based solutions that fail to address root causes.

Conclusion: The Path Forward

The debate between NPA-A and NPA-R reflects genuine strategic dilemmas facing revolutionary movements in contemporary conditions. However, the balance of historical evidence and theoretical analysis supports the "open" approach advocated by NPA-A.

The NFP represents a qualitatively different formation from the Popular Fronts that classical revolutionary theory correctly opposed. Its exclusion of bourgeois parties, its defensive character against far-right threats, and its provision of platforms for revolutionary intervention create opportunities that principled revolutionaries should embrace rather than reject.

The alternative approach advocated by NPA-R, while maintaining certain revolutionary principles, leads toward sectarian isolation that serves bourgeois interests by keeping revolutionary forces marginal and ineffective. The historical record demonstrates that such approaches consistently fail to build significant revolutionary capacity or contribute to mass struggles.

Contemporary conditions—the crisis of traditional social democracy, the growth of far-right movements, the deepening ecological crisis—create both urgent needs for revolutionary intervention and opportunities for building broader anti-capitalist consciousness. Revolutionary organizations that fail to engage with these immediate challenges risk becoming irrelevant to the struggles that will shape the future.

The true revolutionary tradition lies not in maintaining abstract purity but in skillfully combining principled commitment to revolutionary objectives with tactical flexibility and willingness to engage in immediate struggles. NPA-A's approach to the NFP exemplifies this tradition and provides a model for revolutionary intervention in contemporary conditions.

Rather than viewing the NPA split as organizational failure, we should understand it as necessary clarification of strategic alternatives. The future of revolutionary socialism depends on the ability to learn from such experiences while developing approaches that can effectively challenge capitalist domination in all its contemporary forms.

The stakes extend far beyond French politics to the global struggle for human liberation. As capitalism intensifies its assault on working people and the environment, revolutionary movements must develop strategies capable of building mass resistance while maintaining their commitment to fundamental transformation. NPA-A's approach provides a promising model for meeting these challenges, while NPA-R's sectarian alternative threatens to leave revolutionary forces isolated and ineffective when they are most needed.

What Matters Is What You're For,
Not What You're Against

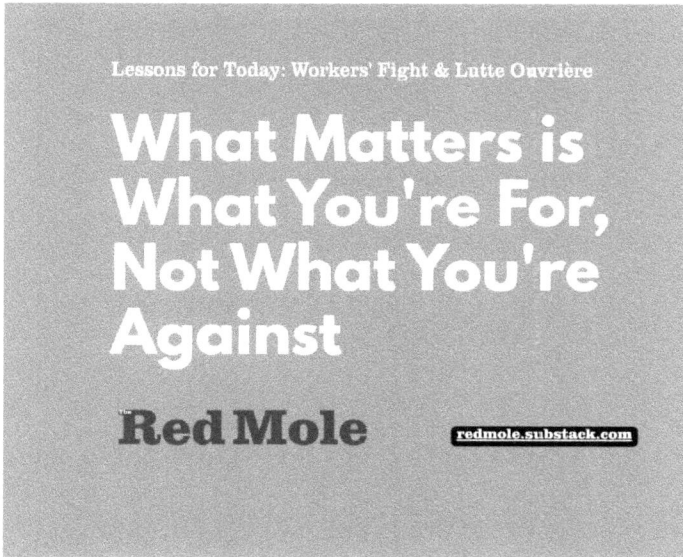

Lessons for Today: Workers' Fight & Lutte Ouvrière

What Matters is What You're For, Not What You're Against

Red Mole

redmole.substack.com

Revolutionary politics often involves sharp criticism of the existing capitalist system, the state, and other political forces, including reformist and even rival revolutionary groups. This is a necessary part of defining one's position. However, historical experiences from Britain and France highlight a crucial lesson for revolutionaries today: simply being against something is insufficient; what truly matters is articulating, implementing, and building the capacity for what you are for. Failure to do so can lead to political ineffectiveness, confusion, and an inability to genuinely guide the working class towards emancipation.

The Pitfall of Just Being "Against"

Critiques of both the British organisation Workers' Fight (WF) and the French organisation Lutte Ouvrière (LO) illustrate the problems of primarily defining oneself by opposition. A critique of Workers' Fight points to the "habitual empty phrasemongering of British Trotskyists," suggesting rhetoric that is long on denunciation but short on substance regarding concrete plans. A key alleged weakness highlighted is the lack of a clear definition of organisational tasks, distinct from political tasks. This relates to the fundamental question of "what is to be done?" While they might be "against" the current state of affairs politically, the practical, organisational steps required to change it are not clearly laid out.

Similarly, Lutte Ouvrière faces repeated criticism for what is described as a "passive critique." LO writes extensively to criticise the actions of other groups, such as the Ligue Communiste Révolutionnaire (LCR), without proposing any alternative line or action themselves. In the context of strikes, LO is criticised for failing to explain how workers should organise after a struggle, on what slogans, and with what forms of struggle to pursue the fight. This is framed as a lack of practical guidance on "how to continue?" Their approach in factory bulletins is described as "economist," focusing on denouncing the failures of bureaucrats and complaining about immediate, even trivial, issues like vending machines or hot water, rather than clearly presenting a revolutionary political alternative and practical steps for change. LO is also seen as reluctant to put forward demands or slogans on their bulletins, reportedly because they do not propose what they cannot personally ensure will be realised. This hesitation highlights a focus on current limitations (against the possibility of immediate victory or full control) rather than a proactive stance on articulating what is needed (for advancing the struggle). This leads to a perceived "sentiment of helplessness" and a contrast with a more active approach to revolutionary intervention.

Beyond these specific groups, the problem is broader. Traditional French parties and unions, like the PCF, CGT, and CFDT, are criticised for being more defined by their integration into the existing system or their verbal opposition than by a clear, revolutionary path forward. The PCF, despite "left" verbalism, is described as having ceased fighting for the revolutionary transformation of society, instead aiming to conquer positions within the existing state. Their positions sometimes fall short of defending workers' immediate interests and may advocate dispersed rather than unified action. The direction of the CFDT is noted for not linking demands strategically (e.g., reduction of work time with salary issues or industrial policy), reflecting a disconnect between different aspects of a positive programme. Established unions can also tend towards "contractual action" over mobilisation and bureaucratic control, stifling initiatives from the base. Even within the Algerian FLN, there was an objective radicalisation, but the organisation itself served as a "catch-all" ('fourre-tout') encompassing both radical and conservative positions, lacking a clear, programmatic "for" beyond the immediate struggle for liberation.

The Necessity of Being "For": Articulating a Programme and Tasks

A revolutionary organisation must define not only what it is against, but crucially, what it is for. This involves:

- Defining Tasks: The critique of Workers' Fight for lacking clear organisational tasks points to the need for revolutionaries to explicitly think through how political goals are to be achieved in practice. The LCR's criticism of LO echoes this, stressing the need for revolutionaries to assume and define organisational tasks and explain how workers should organise. This goes beyond general calls for action and requires concrete planning.

- Developing a Programme and Strategy: Being "for" implies a programme—a set of demands and a strategy to achieve them. The importance of linking immediate demands with broader transitional or socialist goals is highlighted. Revolutions are not achieved by simply defending immediate interests; revolutionaries must articulate a path that moves from present struggles towards the goal of overthrowing capitalism and building socialism. The LCR criticises LO for failing to integrate the conscious role of the revolutionary organisation in proposing alternative tactics and guiding the fight within mass struggles. Demands and slogans must be linked to practical intervention.
- Active Intervention and Mobilisation: A clear "for" requires active intervention. Calls for action are often only possible "at the place of action," suggesting a limitation in their ability to initiate or sustain broader, organised efforts. In contrast, revolutionaries must be capable of intervening in struggles, proposing concrete actions and forms of organisation. This is not just about being present, but about providing leadership and guidance. As the LCR argues against LO, focusing on criticising bureaucrats without proposing alternative tactics is insufficient.
- Educating and Leading: Being "for" involves actively educating the working class. Revolutionaries cannot rely solely on the spontaneous development of consciousness. They must bring political knowledge to workers and explain complex political differences and their practical implications. The role of the revolutionary organisation is to be "a step ahead of the masses," clarifying the path forward rather than adapting to the "average worker's" current level of consciousness.
- Building the Organisation: Ultimately, being "for" requires building a revolutionary organisation capable of implementing the programme and leading the struggle. This involves not just recruiting but training militants, diffusing knowledge, and establishing local structures. It requires a clear political line and the ability to differentiate it from reformist strategies.

Lessons from the FSLN and Challenges for Revolutionaries Today

The example of the Sandinista National Liberation Front (FSLN) in Nicaragua offers a contrasting perspective on being "for." The FSLN presented a "Plan of Struggle" as their programme for the people. They developed a "guide for the propagandist" to instruct militants on how to explain the programme, respond to counter-arguments from counter-revolutionaries, and emphasise assuming errors while presenting the Plan as a way for the people themselves to overcome problems with the FSLN's mobilisation. They explicitly linked the programme to their history of struggle and practical action through house visits and discussions. This demonstrates a conscious effort to articulate what they were for and actively engage the population in that vision.

For current revolutionaries, including those associated with the LCR tradition (which itself faced debates on how to fully articulate its "for" in certain areas, such as self-management theory or addressing new issues like ecology), the lesson is to avoid the trap of defining oneself primarily by opposition. While critique is essential, it must serve the purpose of advancing a clear, practical, and inspiring vision of the future and the steps needed to achieve it. This requires constant theoretical work, strategic planning, self-criticism, and a deep engagement with the practical struggles of the working class, not just observing or criticising them. The ability to explain what we are for and how we plan to get there, rather than merely denouncing what is wrong, is the key to building a genuinely revolutionary movement.

FURTHER READING

For those wishing to delve deeper into the historical experiences discussed and the source materials, the following French documents offer valuable insights:

"Le guide du propagandiste du Front" (The Front's Propagandist Guide): This excerpt details the practical methods used by FSLN militants in Nicaragua to explain their Plan of Struggle (see the English translation in October 1, 1984, Intercontinental Press) to the population. It provides arguments to counter "counter-revolutionary lies" and highlights the importance of an open but firm approach, capable of self-criticism and sensitive to the people's questions. The guide includes concrete suggestions for discussions during house visits and underscores the electoral campaign's significance as an opportunity to develop political consciousness and popular self-organisation. A related excerpt shows the FSLN specifically addressing women, detailing revolutionary gains for children and addressing women's own demands for equality, linking the programme to practical action like house visits. This document exemplifies an organisation consciously articulating and disseminating what it is for.

Texts on the CFDT Debate: "CFDT: des forces importantes pour redresser la barre" (CFDT: Important Forces to Right the Ship): These articles (and for a summary, see Critique Communiste) report on internal opposition within the CFDT trade union confederation, particularly critiquing the leadership's "recentering" towards integrating its action within a "durable capitalist system." Texts from the Basse-Normandie region and the Hacuitex federation reject the fundamental choices of the confederation, advocating for a class and mass unionism ("syndicalisme de classe et de masse") and explicitly calling for unity of action, primarily with the CGT, despite divergences, in the perspective of mobilising workers and pursuing an anti-capitalist struggle. This highlights a debate within a major workers' organisation over defining what it should be for in strategic terms.

"Lutte ouvrière" et la révolution mondiale ("Lutte Ouvrière" and the World Revolution): This document offers a critique of Lutte Ouvrière's (LO) analysis of revolutionary processes internationally. It examines LO's method of analysis and its implications, particularly concerning the nature of revolutions and state power in China, Cuba, and the popular democracies of Eastern Europe. The critique suggests theoretical and practical deviations in LO's approach, which, from the perspective of the analysis presented, hindered a clear understanding of the international revolutionary dynamic.

Critiques of Lutte Ouvrière's Practice and Theory in lutte ouvrière" ou la tendance prolétarienne": This comprehensive analysis delves into the structure and political practice of Lutte Ouvrière, contrasting it with the approach of the Ligue Communiste (LC/LCR). It critiques LO's system of press, particularly its factory bulletins, which are described as often focusing on immediate, even trivial, issues ("économiste") and lacking clear political slogans or alternative actions. The text highlights LO's perceived "passive critique" of other organisations and bureaucrats without proposing alternative lines or explaining how workers should organise or continue struggles. It points to a hesitation in defining specific organisational tasks and a tendency towards a "sentiment of helplessness" when struggles face difficulties. The critique suggests this approach focuses on what LO cannot immediately ensure rather than actively proposing and fighting for necessary steps. The document argues for the revolutionary organisation's necessity to assume and define organisational tasks and bring political knowledge to workers. It also touches upon LO's relationship with student movements.

"Construire le parti, construire l'Internationale" (Building the Party, Building the International): These documents stem from the preparatory debate for the founding congress of the Ligue Communiste. They are dedicated to the theory and system of organisation (Part 1) and the relationship between internationalism and the International (Part 2). These titles themselves indicate a focus on the active construction of the revolutionary instrument, defining the practical tasks required to achieve the revolutionary goal—explicitly outlining what the organisation is for in terms of its structure and international role.

"Pédagogie et crise de la bourgeoisie" (Pedagogy and Crisis of the Bourgeoisie): Authored by the teaching cell of the Ligue Communiste in Toulouse, this brochure analyses the education system within the context of the capitalist state. It critiques reformist approaches to education, including those from the PCF and certain union tendencies, highlighting their limitations in challenging the fundamental function of the school under bourgeois rule. The document aims to provide a basis for revolutionary militants in defining their line of struggle within the education sector, outlining orientations for transforming pedagogy and fighting the crisis of the bourgeoisie as it affects schooling.

"Fascisme et démocratie. Les formes de domination de l'état capitaliste. Suivi de Bonapartisme et fascisme" (Fascism and Democracy. Forms of Domination of the Capitalist State. Followed by Bonapartism and Fascism): This document provides a foundational Marxist theoretical analysis of different forms of the capitalist state, including bourgeois democracy, Bonapartism, and Fascism, including classic texts by Leon Trotsky on the subject. Understanding the nature of the state is crucial for revolutionaries to define what they are against (the capitalist state) and also implicitly shapes their understanding of what they are for (a workers' state, socialism), by defining the structures of domination that must be overthrown.

Critiques of the French Communist Party (PCF): See Critique communiste n°22, Février-Mars 1978 These excerpts include a discussion on the evolution of the PCF and the "Stalinist system," particularly focusing on the PCF's perceived "sectarian turn" after September 1977. One article is titled "PCF: the impossible strategy." Critiques of the PCF's positions, such as regarding a "capitalist private sector" within "advanced democracy" or their general political line, highlight the perceived lack of a viable revolutionary strategy. This serves as an example of a major political force whose strategy is analysed and found wanting from a revolutionary perspective, underscoring the need for revolutionaries to articulate a concrete alternative for achieving socialism.

www.ingramcontent.com/pod-product-compliance
Lightning Source LLC
Chambersburg PA
CBHW042247040426
42334CB00044B/3098